MEMOIRS OF A BLACK PSYCHIATRIST

Memoirs of a
Black Psychiatrist

A Life of Advocacy for Social Change

James L. Curtis

Published in the United States of America by
Michigan Publishing
Manufactured in the United States of America

DOI: http://dx.doi.org/10.3998/mpub.9888120

ISBN 978-1-60785- 431-9 (paper)
ISBN 978-1-60785-432-6 (e-book)

An imprint of Michigan Publishing, Maize Books serves the publishing needs of the University of Michigan community by making high-quality scholarship widely available in print and online. It represents a new model for authors seeking to share their work within and beyond the academy, offering streamlined selection, production, and distribution processes. Maize Books is intended as a complement to more formal modes of publication in a wide range of disciplinary areas.
http://www.maizebooks.org

Dedicated to Viola Wertheim Bernard (1907–1998),
one of the leaders in desegregating American psychiatry
and in establishing community psychiatry as a field
combining public health and psychiatry.

CONTENTS

Being Black in America

Two great African-Americans, with diametrically opposed points of view on the best way to advance the future of their people in this land, dominated black leadership during the 20th century; the dichotomy between strategic methods and tactics can still be seen today.

The first of these was Booker T. Washington (1856–1915) who, in my view, brought about more tangible and massive change than any other black leader before or since. Born a slave on a small farm in Virginia, he went to work in the salt furnaces and coal mines of West Virginia following Emancipation. After receiving a rudimentary elementary education, he briefly tried his hand at studying first the law and then the ministry, but went on to a more satisfying career as a teacher at Hampton Institute. That experience inspired him to help build, along a similar model, the Tuskegee Institute, devoted primarily to producing skilled craftsmen—who actually built and outfitted the buildings of that institution. With the financial support of leading American captains of industry, Tuskegee had become the best-supported black educational institution in the nation by 1900.

In his famous Atlanta Compromise oration in 1895, Washington endeared himself to white leadership in both North and South by proclaiming that the recently freed slaves should postpone their pursuit of equal citizenship rights with white Americans and remain in the rural South. There they would gradually free themselves from their subjugated sharecropping subsistence by first becoming God-fearing obedient farmers, then landowners, then skilled craftsmen and, eventually, small business owners in their segregated communities, thereby escaping the violent wrath of whites who were determined not to grant them their civil rights. Through his extensive speaking tours and his acclaimed autobiography, *Up from Slavery,* Washington attracted tremendous financial support not only from the wealthiest Americans, such as John D. Rockefeller and Andrew Carnegie, but also from lesser-known millionaires, many of whose homes he visited secretly as a personal guest. His celebrated invitation to have lunch with President Theodore Roosevelt inflamed white Southerners, but he continued to be the chief black advisor for Presidents Roosevelt and William Howard Taft. His wealthy Northern white supporters donated personal funds for elementary schools and black teachers in Southern states, although they provided little more than a few months of schooling when youngsters were not needed for farm work. One such philanthropist was Julius Rosenwald, co-owner of Sears and Roebuck and a member of the board of trustees of Tuskegee; with his own money Rosenwald established close to 5,000 elementary schools, more than 200 homes for teachers, and almost 700 "shop" (i.e., vocational training) buildings in 883 counties in 15 Southern states, providing schooling for almost a third of the black children in that region. Moreover, he stipulated that communities where those schools were to be located had to raise a matching amount of money from private sources in order to receive his funding. Although he publicly avoided black activism, Washington privately contributed funds for legal actions opposing the suppression of black voting rights, and he served on the boards of directors of leading black colleges and universities like Howard University in Washington, D.C., and Fisk University in Nashville, both of which provided more elite educational opportunities for blacks. In fact, it is said that he directed almost all of the philanthropic support of American black colleges and universities, and pushed them to produce graduates who were skilled tradesmen as well as professionals, so they need not support themselves solely by their preferred callings.

THIS APPROACH WAS ANATHEMA to William Edward Burghardt Du Bois (1868–1963). Born in Great Barrington, a small town in Massachusetts, he was raised by a single mother after being abandoned early in life by a father he did not know. His parents were free-born blacks. Few blacks lived in Great Barrington, so Du Bois attended the same schools as white children, where he excelled in his studies. It rankled that his academic success would ordinarily have earned Du Bois a scholarship to Harvard University. Instead, members of his childhood church raised the money for him to go to Fisk, and it was there that he spent his summers teaching black children in the Southern countryside, for the first time becoming aware of what it was like to be a black person in this nation. A white professor at Fisk helped him with special tutoring and personal financial support to enroll as an undergraduate at Harvard (which did not accept Fisk credits). After earning a bachelor's degree from Harvard in 1891, Du Bois became the first African-American to receive a PhD from that institution in 1895. A fellowship from the John T. Slater Foundation for the Education of Freedmen enabled him to do graduate work at the University of Berlin, where he studied under some of the greatest social scientists of the age.

When Du Bois returned to the United States, he could find no appointment at a white college or university because of his race, so he accepted a faculty position at all-black Wilberforce University in Ohio. Shortly thereafter, a fellowship from a wealthy white philanthropist enabled him to go to the University of Pennsylvania as an assistant instructor and to study the black segregated community of Philadelphia, which resulted in one of the first scientific sociological studies produced in the nation (*The Philadelphia Negro*, 1899). Deeply disturbed by American racism, North as well as South, Du Bois joined a small group of other well-educated blacks in 1905 to form the Niagara Movement, which met on the Canadian side of Niagara Falls because American hotels did not accommodate blacks in that era. It was meant to be an activist group bringing public awareness to race prejudice and discrimination, but it had no significant financial support or following and did not survive.

In reaction to the Springfield, Illinois, riot in 1909 against blacks who were demanding their civil rights, and which claimed several lives, Du Bois was one of a small group of blacks and many more prominent whites who established the National Association for the Advancement of Colored People (NAACP), whose mission was to insure the political, educational, social, and economic equality of all persons and to eliminate racial hatred and racial discrimination. Among its founders were wealthy and prominent whites, many of whom were from families which formed the American movement for the abolition of slavery; several prominent university faculty members; a number of socialists, and many prominent American Jewish community leaders. Du Bois was the only black member of the NAACP executive committee and, as its director of publications, was the editor of *The Crisis* magazine, which reported monthly on the national racial scene. It was not until 1975 that a black person held the position of president of the NAACP, which was kept alive mainly by white philanthropy, but that organization was the primary voice for equality for AfricanAmericans, and its legal strategy led to the unanimous decision of the United States Supreme Court in 1954 which outlawed the "separate but equal" precedent established by the infamous 1897 *Plessy v. Ferguson* decision, which had led to the legal basis for a Jim Crow America. But the general American public was not ready to make African-Americans full citizens in 1954, just as the American public was not ready in 1865 to accept the so-called Slave Amendments to the U.S. Constitution following the Civil War—the Thirteenth, which abolished slavery; the Fourteenth, which guaranteed due process and equal protection under the laws to all persons, and the Fifteenth, which prohibited racial discrimination in voting rights. After federal troops were withdrawn from the South following the Reconstruction Era, those constitutional guarantees become meaningless words by legal subterfuge, and the North and South united in a national interest to make the United States one of the strongest nations on Earth. Black people, most of whom lived in the South, were reduced to Southern peonage and "slavery by another name."

Du Bois led a tortured life, which in retrospect was marked by more failure than success, despite his undeniable position as the most outstanding intellectual leader of black Americans during his lifetime. In my opinion he believed fundamentally that blacks could never receive full or equal American citizenship, and could never become fully integrated into American society. As early as the 1890s, he rejected the position of the first great American black leader, Frederick Douglass, who had broken ranks even with leading American abolitionists, and had worked hard to convince President Abraham Lincoln finally to accept blacks as soldiers, allow them to fight in the Civil War, and go on to become fully assimilated into American society, socially and in every other way. Essentially, both Douglass and Lincoln believed that the Preamble to the American Constitution expressing the national idea of "freedom and justice for all" represented the true spiritual aspiration of all Americans more forcefully than the Constitution itself, which had been finally endorsed as a compromise between the slaveholding and free states. Du Bois felt it possible that black people could both accept and maintain their racial identity and separateness and (still) become equal Americans. He never abandoned this pessimistic evaluation of the nation. In the 1930s, Du Bois startled the

NAACP by saying that "separate but equal" was an acceptable approach for African-Americans, so long as it was voluntarily chosen rather than imposed upon them. He refused to recant or withdraw that stance, and it was this that led to his resignation/dismissal from the NAACP. For the next ten years, as a professor at black Atlanta University, he led the production of a series of scholarly contributions on African-American life. A personality clash with the president of that institution led to his return to the NAACP for a few years, but again he broke ranks with their racial integration agenda and resigned.

Du Bois was, however, not convinced (at that time) that he should embrace Soviet Communism, and also did not believe white American labor unions would (ever) become willing to admit blacks to full membership. After World War II broke out, he became increasingly committed to Soviet Communism (and) to lose faith in the possibility that the United States would ever give full citizenship rights to blacks. In October 1961, at the age of 93, Du Bois joined the Communist Party and took up residence in Ghana, where he died in 1963, a day before Martin Luther King gave his famous "I Have a Dream" speech at the March on Washington. Du Bois basically refused to recognize the significant achievement of the 1954 *Brown v. Board of Education* decision by the U.S. Supreme Court outlawing "separate but equal" public schools and other vestiges of Jim Crow, or the magnificent civil rights movement of the 1960s, led by Martin Luther King, Jr. and a national coalition of Americans of all religious and ethnic and social class leadership demanding that we become a more inclusive nation. While his militant confrontation with our national racism is praiseworthy, the practical results of this opposition pale in comparison with the concrete building of schools, colleges, and universities for the education of black people in the United States. The chief teachers, professors, and college administrators (of these black colleges) were (for almost a century) almost all white graduates of the nation's leading schools—those schools, though, produced black graduates of distinction who did indeed (in just the past few decades) integrate into the mainstream of the U.S. educational institution.

AS I REFLECT ON this history, I can identify four pathways that a self-respecting and intelligent African-American can personally choose in determining how best to become a full and completely equal American citizen:

1. Confront racist oppression frontally and bravely and never accept compromise or defeat; this is my view of the position of Du Bois, who also held that national racism and international racism had to be addressed with equal intensity, the truth of which I find undeniable.

2. Recognize that, faced with brutal and overwhelming power, striking the best compromise and leaving both black people and their oppressors feeling they have won a partial victory, and that this nonviolent approach to the resolution of human conflict is the best winning strategy in both the short and long term (a view I believe was held by Douglass, Booker T. Washington, King, and even the post-Mecca Malcolm X; the latter two were both assassinated).

3. Retreat into the role of a Christ-like figure who demonstrates the virtue of not answering evil with evil but instead with forgiveness, while dreaming of glory in an afterlife.

4. Forge a creative blend of all the above, depending on the time, the situation, and the possibility of a coalition with other oppressed members of society. This position is best regarded in my view as being in the spirit of American pragmatism, a belief that the best strategy is whatever works best to achieve the desired aim, at a specific time, place, and historical situation with which one must deal.

We have learned from social anthropology since the 1940s that in many ways we are like all human beings who have ever lived; that in many other ways we are like some groups more than others (based on our age, sex, race, religion, and social class); but that each of us is also a unique individual, unlike any other human being who has ever lived. We all embrace different identities at different times and places and in different circumstances, and we have only limited control over the choices we make, most of which are outside our awareness. Cognitive behavioral therapy teaches us that for some persons looking at the same glass of water, it may appear to be half full, while for others looking at the same glass, it will appear to be half empty, and that logically both optimists and pessimists are correct. Moreover, even if the glass is 90 percent full and 10 percent empty, it will feel to some people that the glass is not full enough—nothing but 100 per cent is the right amount for them—while even 10 percent will give optimists some cause for hope that eventually times will improve. Clearly, we cannot all be in the first category all the time; nor can all of us be our parents' favored or only child; nor can our family or kin control everything in view. This is what makes human life interesting, unpredictable, and a challenge for us all.

It has been my good fortune in life to have grown up with a circle of family and community supports, which allowed me to live a life full of both accomplishment and failure. As I tell the story of important highlights in my career, I am fully aware that many successes were the result of good choices I made, but more often it was a matter of luck and being on the right side of the history of our national struggle to become a more just and equitable society. I confess that I also quite often had no idea what was happening or why. A life of success still has many failures: the great sports idol Babe Ruth hit 714 home runs, but he also struck out 1,330 times.

ACKNOWLEDGMENTS

The book was written in stages from the year 2003 to the current 2017 year. I received important guidance on early drafts from Laura Lein, John Tropman, and Linda Cashdan; on later drafts from Jeff Mortimer, David Heleniak, and Terrance McDonald. I appreciate also the careful guidance and support from Jaclyn Sipovic and Patrick Goussy in producing the book. To the many others who encouraged me to continue work on the book I am deeply grateful.

My Life

Chapter one deals with the earliest years of my life, after my parents left the rural South in the first wave of the Great Migration, and through high school. Chapter two covers the Albion College and University of Michigan Medical School years, when the Jim Crow mentality still prevailed in the land. Chapter three recounts my service in the military, not as an Army private serving in a segregated unit in 1943, but in the Air Force, which had been desegregated by an executive order of President Harry Truman, a Southerner who defied his early upbringing and the dire predictions of U.S. military leadership, which was largely made up of Southern whites. In 1952 I was Chief of Psychiatry at the hospital at Mitchel Air Force Base on Long Island, which was racially integrated for officers and their families as well as enlisted men and their families. Since I aspired to a career in academic medicine, I was also a faculty member at the State University of New York Downstate Medical Center in Brooklyn. It was during this time that my young family experienced the first of many tragedies when our first child, Larry, was found to be autistic and mentally handicapped. My successful leadership involvement in the Brooklyn black community of Bedford-Stuyvesant fueled my commitment to increasing the enrollment of blacks in racially integrated higher education.

Chapter four covers my 12 years at Cornell Medical College, where I was called to become a member of the dean's staff, an associate professor of psychiatry, and a national leader as affirmative action began to desegregate American medical education. Cornell went on to become an outstanding example of integrated medical education. Chapter five covers the 18-year period after I left Cornell to become a clinical professor of psychiatry at the Columbia

University College of Physicians and Surgeons, and head of the Department of Psychiatry at Harlem Hospital Center, serving one of the largest black ghetto communities in the nation. My retirement in 2000 begins Chapter six. My return to my home town of Albion, Mich., in 2003, coincided with the progression of my late wife Vivian's Alzheimer's disease, which left her totally impaired and requiring nursing home care until her death in August 2007. Four months later, my second son, Paul, died suddenly of a massive heart attack after many years of serious psychiatric illness, which snuffed out the promise he had shown in his first year as a law student at Harvard.

These retirement years have been among the most rewarding of my life as I have been able to give back many of my resources to the Albion community to help bring new life into a town almost destroyed by the decline of the domestic automobile industry. My contributions to the University of Michigan, from whose medical school I graduated in 1946 as the only black in a class of 145, and from whose school of social work Vivian graduated in 1948, have been particularly significant. Both of us appreciated the important role of the university, not only in our own lives but in the lives of all underrepresented minority groups and of women, in expanding opportunity for all people to make our country a more complete and equal land. Most of our estate has been left to the University of Michigan to express our personal commitment to join and strengthen this great institution in our shared mission.

My life story expresses my personal set of choices at various times of my life to make the best of historical opportunities presented to me to help build a more completely inclusive American society. It is unlikely that any other person born at my particular time and place and station in life could have traveled this identical life pathway because we are all unique, like different snowflakes, no two of which are believed to be exactly alike, during a brief lifetime of existence.

CHAPTER I

The Formative Years
Childhood through High School, 1922–1940

ABOLISHING SLAVERY MEANT WIPING out a highly successful capitalist enterprise. In 1790, the South produced only 1,000 tons of cotton. By 1860, it was producing a million tons annually. Over the same time span, the number of slaves in the United States grew from 700,000 to four million. Slavery was maintained by brute force: in 1860, the state of Virginia, with a total population of 1.2 million, had a military force of more than 100,000 men, almost a tenth of the population, to keep things under control. The U.S. Civil War claimed at least 620,000 lives, about 3% of the population, making it by far our deadliest war. But it is seldom realized that two-thirds of whites in the South owned no slaves. A few thousand wealthy planters made $50 million in 1850, while all other families in the South combined earned only $60 million. The great majority of whites were poor, barely surviving by subsistence farming or working in some form of law enforcement that allowed them to exploit the privilege of being white. The end of slavery left all Southerners almost as impoverished as the newly freed blacks.

The population of the nation grew from 31 million to 75 million between 1860 and 1900; 20 million of those people lived west of the Mississippi. The number of farms tripled, from two million to six million. Farming was becoming increasingly mechanized: there were steel plows, mowing machines, reapers, harvesters, improved cotton gins, and giant combines that cut grain, threshed it, and bagged it. A great expanse of land and machines was leaving many small farmers at the mercy of virtually unregulated banks and railroads.

It wasn't long before only a small number of large landowners could thrive agriculturally.

With the end of Reconstruction and the withdrawal of Union troops from the South in 1877, the recently freed slaves quickly lost the essential protections provided by the Thirteenth, Fourteenth, and Fifteenth Amendments to the Constitution, as well as the Civil Rights Act of 1875 that outlawed racial discrimination, whether public or private. American historian Rayford Logan has dubbed the period from 1876 to 1900 the nadir of the history of blacks in this country.

My parents were born in the midst of those tragic years, my mother in 1890 and my father in 1896, in the small farm village of Jeffersonville, Georgia, about 50 miles from Macon. My father served during World War I as a private in a labor battalion, an assignment given to almost all black soldiers in the U.S. Army. On his return to Jeffersonville, he and about 20 of his friends eagerly responded to an offer of factory work in the North. An official from the Albion Malleable Iron Company was recruiting black men to move to Albion, Michigan, a small town of about 8,000 that was 95 miles west of Detroit, the capital of an automobile industry so prosperous that factories were springing up all through the surrounding country. Following the lead of Henry Ford, automakers had been recruiting immigrants to work for them since around the turn of the century. After the outbreak of World War I, immigrant labor was not allowed into the country, and blacks from the South became a new labor source. Albion Malleable recruited a group of blacks from Pensacola, Florida, in 1916, and then began seeking workers in small villages in other parts of the South. Just as Ford had done in Detroit, Albion Malleable not only provided jobs, but also built company houses that the men could buy. The workers also had access to year-round public schools for their children, and a whole new, freer way of life. Thus it was that in 1922 my father came to Albion, which soon had 800 blacks in its population of 8,000. My mother and I—I was then nine months old—joined him a few months later. We moved into a company house that my father planned to own eventually.

These black newcomers to the urban Midwest did not get a warm welcome from everyone. Many native-born white Protestants wanted a 100 percent white America. The Ku Klux Klan spread from the South to infect many Northern communities. D. W. Griffith's legendary, notorious, and hugely popular 1915 movie, *The Birth of a Nation,* portrayed blacks during Reconstruction as brutal savages bent on destroying white civilization and debauching white womanhood. It was shown at the White House by President Woodrow Wilson. The Klan also despised Catholics, Jews, and immigrants. Not only blacks, but also poor whites from the South had migrated north to work in the booming factories. Many of them flocked to the banner of the Klan, as did a number of prominent and well-educated northern Protestants. Many smaller Michigan towns had strong local branches and, by 1924, Detroit had an estimated 35,000 Klansmen, who had become a powerful political bloc. Racially segregated neighborhoods were almost universal throughout the North.

In 1925, a black physician in his late 20s, Dr. Ossian Sweet, moved into a corner bungalow home in an all-white Detroit neighborhood with his wife, Gladys, and their three-year-old daughter. A graduate of Wilberforce, the black college near Xenia, Ohio, Dr. Sweet earned his MD at Howard University, the more prestigious of the two black medical schools in the country, and then did a year of postgraduate work in Paris and Vienna, like many other American physicians who sought the best training in the world at the time.

Both he and his wife were better educated and more socially polished than their neighbors, but they were harassed, threatened, and intimidated from the time they moved in, with the intent of frightening them into flight. They had anticipated this, and they were determined to defend their right to live where they chose rather than run. Threats and rumors spread by the Klan forced them to call on the local police for protection. About a dozen officers came to the neighborhood; among them, it was believed, were several Klansmen. The harassment and threats continued, and after several more nights of these assaults, Dr. Sweet asked 11 of his black male friends to come to his home, armed and ready to fight back if they were attacked. Stones were thrown through their window, and a number of cars filled with whites surrounded the house. The black men inside the house fired several warning shots, one of which killed a white policeman. All 12 black men were arrested, charged and tried for murder. The local and national offices of the NAACP enlisted several of the best lawyers in the country to defend them. Clarence Darrow led the legal team, first through a mistrial, and then to an acquittal that affirmed their right not to be hounded down and killed in their own homes.

During my elementary school years, 1927 to 1934, Albion was at least as racially segregated as many other nearby towns, if not more so. We lived on the northwest side, near the Malleable Iron Company. Most of the houses there had been built by the foundry; they initially housed immigrant white workers, blacks later joined them as their neighbors. The two groups got along well with each other, but maintained separate churches and taverns. All of these houses had been built without electricity, indoor plumbing, or central heating; the owners had to pay for those niceties themselves. On the southwest side of Albion, across the Michigan Central Railway track and the Kalamazoo River, most blacks lived in a more segregated pattern. The West Ward School, originally built primarily for the children of immigrant German workers but later turned into an all-black elementary school, was located there, as were the town's three black churches. All the other neighborhoods were essentially white, and public accommodations such as hotels, restaurants, beer halls, and barber shops were off-limits for blacks unless they worked there. Even the cemetery was segregated, with immigrant ethnic groups on one of its borders, next to the blacks, and the rest of the plots reserved for whites.

Because the West Ward School did not have a kindergarten, all the five-year-olds on my side of town went to the Austin School a mile away. After kindergarten, all black children who lived on or west of Albion Street, where I lived, were sent to West Ward School for first grade. All white children living anywhere on the north side attended Austin School for all their elementary school years. Only a few black children who lived nearby continued at Austin School after kindergarten.

Although neither of my parents had gone beyond fifth grade in Georgia, they both read the local daily newspaper as well as the black weekly newspapers that had a nationwide circulation, especially the *Chicago Defender* and *Pittsburgh Courier*. I already knew the alphabet and numbers up to 100 when I entered kindergarten, and I could also write them and was beginning to read. The Austin School teachers decided that I was a child of above average ability and that I should remain there rather than being transferred to West Ward. They explained to my mother that it was in my best interest that I remain at Austin, and it was my preference as well. Thus, I spent all of my elementary school years there, while my two younger brothers and my sister went to West Ward after their kindergarten year. This annoyed West Ward's black female principal, who made several visits to discuss the matter with my mother.

Some of my happiest memories are of kindergarten. The teacher was very fond of me, and I must admit that I enjoyed being her "pet." At the end of the afternoon, after we had taken our nap, she would gather us around her in a circle and read one of the classic stories for children: "Goldilocks and the

Three Bears," "The Three Little Pigs," "Little Red Riding Hood," and my special favorite, "Little Black Sambo."

In the evening, after dinner, with my mom sitting above us in her rocking chair, I would gather my younger brothers Tom and Uly (short for Ulysses) and our little sister Gertrude in a semicircle with me as I shared the children's story our teacher had read to us that day. My memory was very good and I believe I repeated them almost word for word, recreating the teacher's tone of voice and the suspense and surprise that it conjured. We all enjoyed these story sessions immensely. I recall with some amused wonder how, in later years, other young black radicals like Malcolm X felt only deep humiliation and insult and died a thousand deaths on hearing "Little Black Sambo," which was written by Helen Bannerman, the wife of an English missionary, for the entertainment of her own children. Though she depicted him as a little black East Indian boy, I simply looked on him as a little black boy like me, and I found it thrilling that he outwitted the tigers, who took away his attractive clothes and then found themselves chasing each other round and round in a circle until they turned into melted butter, which he took home for his mom to use in making pancakes for him and his parents. "Little Black Sambo" was banished from libraries and had to go into hiding during the 1960s, a casualty of Black Pride, but, to me, his self-confidence and cunning far surpassed all three pigs as well as Little Red Riding Hood.

Why West Ward School existed was a subject of much discussion in Albion's black community. The favored theory was that some of the early black arrivals were accustomed to segregated schools with black teachers and had aspirations that some of their children would hold jobs as teachers there in the future, since there were no college graduates among them at that time. In 1917, white school officials from Albion went to nearby Hillsdale College, which was graduating two black students, a young woman who was interested in teaching at the segregated black school and a young man who became principal of that school in 1920. They, in turn, recruited two more young black women to teach, both of whom were graduating from Michigan State Normal College (now Eastern Michigan University).

For many years, I thought it was a great mistake to have such a segregated school, but I later understood that many of the black children coming from the South who were 10 or 12 years old had only had one or two years of school but were much too old to be in a class of 6- or 7-year-olds. Regrettably but understandably, this also meant that teaching and learning would move at a slower pace. And blacks from the South, who had only known segregated schools, felt pride in having black teachers in those schools. But the situation still disadvantaged black youngsters of above average ability—of whom there were quite a few—who attended West Ward School. After they completed sixth grade, all Albion students, black and white, went on to the same junior and senior high school. Several of my friends and relatives who came from West Ward confided in me that it took them one or two years to compensate for their less-adequate preparation.

I was one of three students at Austin School who finished our assignments so much faster than the other students that we were given added work. Daryl Sebastian, Peter Lazarchuk, and I were given extra books to read, or reports to make on either encyclopedia articles or topics we selected ourselves. I never understood why neither Daryl nor Peter continued to excel in high school; neither went on to college, as far as I know. Ethnic whites from immigrant families, as well as working-class and lower-class whites who were born in this country, did not automatically think of attending college after graduating from high school in that era. But many black families valued education highly and in the 1920s one Albion family sent two of their daughters to Talladega College in Alabama, one of the most highly regarded black colleges in those years. The oldest one moved from Albion to Detroit, where she taught chemistry in high school; the younger daughter remained in Albion after finishing college and taught at the segregated West Ward elementary school.

My father died of pneumonia in February 1930, when I was in second grade. I was the oldest of their four surviving children. He and my mother had married in 1920, when she was 30 and he was 24; it was her second marriage and his first. Their first child, a girl, died of influenza shortly after being born. She was my father's first child, and he took her death very hard. Perhaps as a result, he showered me with affection after I came along, always wanting to hold me on his knee and kiss me, which annoyed my mother because she was afraid he would spoil not only me, but my two younger brothers and baby sister Gertrude. He had lots of love and hugs and kisses for all of us. There was about a year and a half in age between each of us.

Many of my father's siblings left Jeffersonville both before and after World War I to live in the larger city of Macon, which offered more jobs and had a rather large and prosperous black middle class. Several of them had more than an elementary school education, and one of my father's nephews, Rufus, was our family's first college graduate, finishing his degree at Tuskegee Institute (now Tuskegee University), the school in Alabama led by Booker T. Washington for its first 34 years.

My father had become a 32nd degree Mason in Albion, and at the time of his death was Worshipful Master of the local black lodge. He also belonged to the Knights of Pythias and the Odd Fellows. He was one of the six founders of the local black chapter of the American Legion, and the members named the post in his honor after he died. He was a church member but, unlike my mother, he rarely attended, and kept his skepticism about religion, churches, and ministers to himself. He played the guitar well, gambled, drank moonshine whiskey he made in a distillery in our cellar, and owned a Model T Ford that he and his friends would often take apart and reassemble during a weekend just for the fun of it. He would have preferred moving all of us to Detroit, where both he and my mother had relatives, but she would have none of it, preferring the relative peace and security of small-town Albion.

My mother's side of the family was more comfortable with the rural Southern lifestyle. Her mother, part Indian and part black, was the common-law wife of a white farmer whose family practically ran the county. He had two sisters and several brothers who apparently accepted the three black children he fathered: my Aunt Fannie, the oldest; my mother, and then my Uncle Alec. He did not have a white wife or family and was probably just considered a headstrong and rebellious young man. I believe he left about 10 acres and several farm animals to each of his black children when he died. My mother was the only one of the three to move north, although most of her siblings' children did so in later years.

After my mother's first marriage, at age 15, had failed, she and her daughter Lucille and son Willie moved back to live with her mother; my mother had two more children, John and Mary, by different men. She brought four of her five children, including me (she had married my father by then), at age nine months, to Albion with her. Her oldest child, Lucille, had married at age 16, and she and her first husband moved to Albion a few months after my mom and the others had come.

Lucille and her husband bought a house near ours, but shortly thereafter their marriage broke up, leaving her with one son close to my age. She was attractive, soon remarried, and had three more children, all of whom spent as much time in our house as they did in their own and called our mother

"Mom" and their mother "Lucille," just as we did. All of my older siblings' children spent considerable time in our home. In many ways, I grew up in a clan rather than a family.

Lucille's second husband, originally from Mississippi, was William Tucker, a World War I veteran who had seen duty in France. He joined one of the black professional baseball teams that toured the country when he returned to the United States. He and several of his teammates had played in Albion and, attracted by the prospect of good factory jobs and pay, decided to leave the team and settle down and have families there. Tucker, as we called him, was well informed on racial matters and politics, and often regaled us with tales of his wartime adventures. He was also a great hunter and fisherman, and became an important father figure for me after I lost mine. During hunting season, he shared with our family some of the rabbits, squirrels, quail, and pheasants that he bagged in a day of hunting with four or five friends. When hunting season was over, he often took me with him for walks in the nearby woods, where we would pick apples, pears, berries, and nuts as he talked about his past. Like my father, Tucker never went to church, and I do not believe he even joined, although Lucille was always active in the church choir. Lucille was like a second mother to me, and she lavished more love and affection on me than on her own children.

Next in age to Lucille was my older brother Willie, whom we called Bud. He was 14 when we came to Albion and was immediately sent to work in the Malleable, which did not pay close attention to child labor laws at that time. He even lived at our home for two years after he married his first wife, Lorraine. She was very fond of me, came from a family with several well-educated members, spoke beautifully, and was my first real teacher. She taught me the alphabet and my numbers and read the comic strips to me every night, from which I learned to read. Bud was a diligent factory worker, an expert grinder who smoothed off the edges of the iron auto parts after they were broken out of their molds. He was meek and mild during the week, but on weekends he was continually intoxicated and high, as well as irritable. He wrecked several cars and served a few short jail sentences for driving under the influence. When their son was born, Bud and Lorraine moved to their own apartment, but their marriage failed a few years later and they both returned to live with their parents. He, too, did not believe in or go to church. It was Bud who taught me to play checkers, and never once did I beat him. When the snow was deep in winter, he would meet me when I got out of school and give me a ride home on his shoulders.

My brother John, almost 13 when he came to Albion, was sent to work in the Malleable after spending a year at Austin School. He also lived with us until he married some years later. John was a bright person who read a great deal, spoke impeccable English, and was generally well informed, not to mention handsome. When it came to card games and, especially, checkers, he was the best in town, unbeatable. Alcohol made him sick to his stomach, so he didn't drink. He soon moved to Detroit, where he saw the advantages of labor unions. On his return to Albion, he led several attempts to organize a labor union in the Malleable. After failing to heed warnings from management to cease this outrage, he was fired and blacklisted, never to be rehired, and shortly thereafter relocated permanently to Detroit. How different his life might have been if he had been given a better deal.

My sister Mary, the youngest of my older siblings, was nine years older than I and 10 years old when she came to live with us in Albion. Mom only allowed her to go to school for two years before removing her so she could help full-time with the many household chores. Mary was an angry child, resentful that she was less attractive than her older sister Lucille, and that she was being deprived of an education. My mother always insisted that she take me with her when she went out on weekends with girls her own age, and I always gave a full account of everything that had happened when we got home. She married at 15, moved into her own apartment, and soon had her daughter Lola, but the marriage was short-lived. She quickly remarried, to a man named Henry Williams, who had been an umpire for the baseball team on which Tucker had played.

While Henry was working in the Malleable one day, a splatter of molten iron blinded him in one eye. Occupational safety wasn't much of a priority in the factories of the day, nor was there any such thing as worker's compensation, but the foundry did employ him for the rest of his working years. Henry was another father figure for me. He was deeply religious, unlike the other older men in the family, and an ordained assistant minister in our church. Mary was frosty and distant, but also very active in the church, especially the choir. She and Henry were the first family members to own a piano, a player piano with rolls of classical music that I played and listened to for hours. Their daughter, Lola, and I took piano lessons from the same teacher.

And since the local movie theater restricted blacks to the last two rows of the balcony, Mary and Henry and Lola would take me with them to nearby Jackson, where the theater allowed blacks to sit anywhere they pleased. The state had passed a strengthened public accommodations law in 1937, but it was ignored in Albion. In fact, Michigan had passed numerous civil rights acts since 1867, when segregation in schools was banned, but these laws also were widely ignored until a new wave of civil rights activity began stirring after World War II.

My father's death changed our lives in many ways. His life insurance policies paid for the modernization of our home. We had a furnace and hot water heater installed, as well as indoor plumbing, freeing us from the outhouse. Electricity replaced kerosene lamps. We were living much better in material terms, but life was sadder without him.

When the holidays came that year, I recited from memory all the beautiful lines of Clement Clarke Moore's classic poem *A Visit from St. Nicholas* in our third grade Christmas program. It was a great hit. The male student teacher from Albion College drove to my mother's home to ask if I could go with him to his fraternity house Christmas party to recite the poem for his frat brothers, and she consented. It was a great show, and I came back with an armful of presents. Our church also had an annual Christmas program put on by the children, a big deal in all black churches, and before a packed house I recited the long poem again, to sustained and thunderous applause. That single event made my name as a rising star in Albion.

The Sunday school superintendent, William Beck, took me under his wing as his special child star. Soon I was going with him to state and regional meetings in our Baptist church conference, where he held offices. He had given me a big book of poems, and whenever there was a lull in the proceedings, he would announce, "And now we will be favored by a poem given by one of my Sunday school students, Master James Curtis." This was heady stuff, and it went on for about four years, at which time Superintendent Beck led a faction that broke away from Macedonia Baptist Church to protest the dictatorial control of the pastor, Reverend William Hunt. My mother was among those who refused to return to Bethel Baptist Church, the biggest of the black churches, which they had left some years earlier when they could not tolerate the high-handed behavior of the pastor there; our family remained at Macedonia. Bill Beck was a remarkable leader, not only in church affairs, but also in the Albion Republican Party. Up until the New Deal of Franklin D.

Roosevelt, almost all blacks were loyal to the party of Abraham Lincoln. Beck was among the first blacks to come to Albion to work in the factory, arriving in 1916 from Pensacola, Fla. Although not college educated, he was well read and informed, and it was he who saw to it that the great black weekly newspapers were widely distributed in Albion. He arranged for me to be the newspaper boy who delivered these papers and collected the money that gave me my first savings bank account at school.

Charles (Doc) Anderson, the Boy Scout master for the black Troop 62, was another great leader for all of us. We always put on a special drill and marching performance for the annual Memorial Day parade. The Boy Scouts law, motto, oath—the whole manual, in fact—rang in my mind and memory from the time I was 12 until I went to college.

BUT THE MAJOR ARCHITECT of my life was my mother, an ingenious girl from the rural South who turned my brothers Tom and Uly, my sister Gertrude, and me into small farmers. Our house was situated on more than an acre of land, part of which she turned into a small garden where we grew string beans, tomatoes, beets, squash, and okra. We also had a chicken coop and yard where we kept about 50 chickens, a small pond with six ducks, and a pig pen with four hogs. Later, during the Depression, the city of Albion gave large plots of land to people who wanted to grow their own food. We must have had about three acres that were plowed and planted with corn, black-eyed peas, and potatoes. As soon as school let out in June, Mom brought us out to the garden to hoe the long rows, getting rid of weeds. Each of us had a row, and she did, too, coaching us on how to do a good job, showing us by example, and helping little sister Gertrude to do her row. Time was left for about two hours of play after dinner. No sooner had we finished hoeing all the rows than it was time to start over again. Our garden was always picture perfect. Some of our neighbors' plots were miserable by comparison; some had no gardens at all. Their children played all summer long. Mom sold many vegetables, eggs, and chickens to those neighbors.

Mom also had strict rules. We were not allowed to cross Austin Avenue, about a quarter of a mile south of our house, where the corner grocery store we patronized was located. Austin Avenue was part of U.S. 12, a major artery with frequently heavy traffic that extended from Detroit (90 miles to the east) to Chicago (200 miles to the west). Our exact whereabouts were known at all times. Each of us had chores to perform both inside and outside the house, and these had to be done well and with a sense of pride. Whether it was vegetables or flowers, grapes or fruit trees, chickens and even occasionally a dozen rabbits, mom knew how to make them grow.

Each spring, she would order 100 chicks shipped to us in several flat cartons, from which we could hear chirping as we brought them to the basement. We had to give them food and water, adjust the lighting by day and night, and keep their area clean. We usually lost only about 10 out of 100 chicks; one of our neighbors was lucky to have 10 grow up. After school reopened in September, we had to start at 5 a.m. to have time to finish the regular chores before going to classes, then went back to work again after school was over. It never occurred to us to object, rebel, or complain. Her strict work discipline was never applied to the children of our older brothers and sisters, who were left to make their own rules for their own offspring. After we became adults, my younger siblings and I agreed that the high expectations and hard work demanded of us had been a major blessing in our lives.

One day when I was in eighth grade, my English teacher, Mrs. Cornwell, asked me to remain after school. She told me that she and some of her colleagues knew that I was a bright student who wanted to go to college, but that my family couldn't afford it. She wanted me to know that, as a group, these teachers had decided that they would finance my college education, so that I need not worry about it. I was overjoyed, of course, and could hardly wait to get home and tell my mom, who was also delighted by the news. As it turned out, I eventually won other scholarships that paid my way, so these teachers never had to provide this money, but I can truthfully say that the offer in and of itself was a most significant gift for which I have always been grateful, and their example has motivated me to help other young students who needed the kind of inspiration, security, and hope that they gave me.

Miss Leitha Perkins was in charge of extracurricular student programs in speech, drama, and debate when I was in ninth grade. (Years later, she and I remained close personal friends.) She confided to me that a white student graduating that year had remarked that he didn't believe that black students in the school were intelligent enough to put on a play of their own, and she had told him she would prove him wrong.

A white playwright named Paul Green had written several beautiful plays about blacks in the Deep South. One of them, *No 'Count Boy,* written in 1925, featured black teenagers. She asked if I would like to play the lead role of the 17-year-old who was running away from home, headed for New York. He was trying to persuade a young girl to leave the farmer she was engaged to and come with him to see Niagara Falls and live in New York City. Not only was he a convincing storyteller, but he played the harmonica like a professional; this was to be one of the means by which he would finance their trip. I could not play the harmonica myself, but one of my friends was quite good at it, and he played off stage as I went through the motions.

The play was a great success, although all of the other cast members were several grades ahead of me. (Incidentally, the title character's mother catches up with him at the end of the play and forces him to return home.) A friend of mine who saw the show said that he had never heard me play the harmonica and couldn't understand how, when I removed it from my mouth at one point, it kept on playing a little longer.

Miss Perkins advised me not to spend time with the drama club because I would be limited to parts as a black servant or some other such stereotype. She said I should go out for the debating team, and I became a leading member throughout my senior high school years. Mr. Norman Cobb replaced her the next year as head of the debate squads and, under his guidance, I became a skillful debater. Miss Perkins, who continued to work with students in speech, urged me to specialize in extemporaneous speaking, since it was more challenging than declamatory speech (in which one recited great orations from the past) or oratory (in which one created and recited an original speech of one's own).

In extemporaneous speaking, all high school students around the country were given a single area of interest for the year; for instance, John L. Lewis and the United Mine Workers. The judges would write the titles of about 50 topics related to the issue on pieces of paper that were folded and put into a box or hat. Each contestant had an hour after drawing his or her topic to prepare a 10-minute speech on it, and the judges decided which speaker had made the most interesting, informative, logical, clear, and concise presentation. Miss Perkins coached me for three years in extemporaneous speaking, and in my senior year, 1940, I won the Southeastern Michigan high school championship for a speech entitled "A Student Looks at the War in Norway." My prizes were a Webster's Collegiate Dictionary with my name embossed in gold on the front, and a banner from the University of Michigan bearing my name and that of Albion High School. I was also selected to be the graduating class orator that year, and my commencement address on the "Philosophy of Democracy" was well received. I was a member of the Honor Society and the

Student Council, and a writer on the school newspaper. My classmates also voted me "most likely to succeed," which was particularly gratifying since there were only nine blacks in our class of 141.

Debating was the activity that brought out the best in me. Here again, all U.S. high school students were given the same area of concern, such as "Should we adopt a unicameral rather than a bicameral legislature?" or "Should there be government ownership and operation of railroads?" or, as World War II loomed, "Should we enter into a military alliance with Great Britain?"

In preparation for competition against other schools, debate team members had to be able to argue the case for both the positive and the negative. Thus, we read many articles in leading newspapers and journals of thought and opinion, learning a great deal not only about current events, but also their historical origins. At practice after school each day, the coach would have us shift both partners and positions. Each of us had boxes of file cards with pertinent quotations from *The New York Times, The Wall Street Journal, Atlantic Monthly, The Nation, The New Republic, Foreign Affairs,* and *The Annals of the American Academy of Political and Social Science.*

My career ambition at the time was to be a lawyer, and all of this was excellent preparation. My forensic activities helped me far more than my regular classroom work did to think, speak, and write with precision and critical judgment. Our team prospered as well. In my senior year, we won the championship of our regional conference, made it to the quarterfinals of the state championships before being eliminated, and won six out of six debates at a tournament in Jackson and three out of four at a tournament in Lansing. Almost half the members of the debate squad were the children of Albion College faculty or other professionals in town.

Albion High's principal, William Harton, thought highly of me and was supportive in many ways, so much so that I felt confident in asking him, one afternoon during my senior year, why he didn't end the practice of racially segregated lockers in our high school, which I thought insulting. He replied frankly that he was under strict orders from the local school board to keep things that way. When I was a high school junior, Mr. Harton selected me to deliver the Gettysburg Address at the grave site of Albion's war heroes as part of Memorial Day ceremonies. He later introduced me to Theodore Van Dellan, an attorney and University of Michigan Law School graduate who was just establishing his practice in our town. He was pleased to be my mentor and certain that I would also go to U-M. Having come from a poor family himself, he warned me that it would not be easy either academically or socially at Michigan because most of the students there were from privileged backgrounds. In 1941, with his encouragement, I organized a branch of the NAACP in Albion and became its president.

GERTRUDE, SIX YEARS MY junior, was a premature baby, weighing only two and a half pounds at birth. Had she been white, she would have been born in the hospital and kept in a special room with an incubator but, just as I had been in Georgia, most black babies were born at home and attended by black midwives who had learned from their mothers how to bring babies into the world. When the midwife reported to the local health department that a child of low birth weight had been born, a white physician was sent to our home each day. The doctor told my mom that the baby would not live long because her lungs had not been well formed before birth. My mom is said to have told the doctor, "With God's help, I will raise this child." She sent her daughter Lucille to the store to buy a large piece of flannel cloth, which she cut into pieces and hemmed to wrap around the infant, placing her in a little box and covering it with a tiny quilt. This served as a homemade incubator.

The physician visited each day and was so surprised to see how the baby was thriving that he brought a different physician with him every day, all of them marveling at how well everything was going. Mom had placed Gertrude near the stove in the dining room to keep her warm, fed her teaspoons of milk when she woke up, kept her body clean and warm and oiled, and massaged her over and over. Gertrude contracted pneumonia when she was three days old and the doctor thought she surely would not survive, but she did. She had pneumonia again at age three but recovered as she had done before. Our Dad died when she was two years old.

She started kindergarten at Austin School when she was five, following which she was transferred to West Ward, as had been the case with my brothers Tom and Uly. Mom had given Tom orders to be sure that nobody picked on Gertrude; he was always big and tough for his age, and nobody ever tried.

I too had the occasion to protect our little sister from disrespectful treatment when she was in fourth grade. Albion College did not send student teachers to West Ward because the curriculum there was not the same as in the predominantly white schools, nor did the students' ages always correspond with their grade levels because children coming from the South often had to be placed in lower grades than their ages would indicate. Nonetheless, students from one of the Albion College sororities formed a girls club at West Ward that met once a week for various fun activities. As Christmas season approached, the sorority girls decided to put together a special program which the West Ward girls would perform for the entire West Ward student body and, later, at the sorority house.

One evening, as I was studying in the little room set off from the living room that I had turned into an office for doing my homework (complete with a set of books my mom had purchased from a door-to-door salesman who convinced us both that I needed them to make me an even better student), I heard Gertrude singing a song that was new to me. "Gertrude," I said, "come here and tell me about this song you're singing." "Oh," she said, "that's the song the college girls are teaching us for our Christmas show." These are the words she was singing: "If every star was a little pickaninny and there was a little chicken in the moon, say there'd be no light 'cause every night, each coon they'd cook him in the dipper on the milky, milky way, and they'd have chicken dinner morning, night and noon; Oh, if every star was a little pickaninny and there was a little chicken in the moon . . ." I said, "Oh no, you won't be singing any insulting song like that at that Christmas party."

When I went to school the next day, I asked the principal if I could speak with the superintendent, who had an office in the same building. I described the situation and explained why I considered it degrading to have those West Ward children singing a song that insulted themselves and all the other black people in town. He said he would take care of it, and apparently he did. The sorority sisters still had a Christmas show, but the West Ward girls sang regular Christmas carols.

In many ways, Gertrude's life followed the same path followed by many other young black girls of that day. When she became pregnant at 16, she tried to hide it from our Mom, who found out anyway when Gertrude stopped having her period and began to show signs of morning sickness. Gertrude admitted she had been going out secretly with a young man eight years older than she, who worked in the Malleable and roomed with a family on our street. Mom called the young man in, who immediately said that he would marry Gertrude, which was what was expected in those days. They obtained a license from the county clerk's office and were married by the young man's landlord, who was also an assistant minister of our church. Their baby boy was stillborn, and they separated a month later. It turned out he was already married, and Gertrude's marriage to him was annulled.

Although she had dropped out of school, she kept her part-time job with a young married couple in their home, which she had had for more than a year. On weekdays, she helped the mother with dinner and getting their two youngsters ready for bed, and then worked all day Saturday while the couple shopped and did other errands. She earned $7.50 a week, all of which she handed over to our mother, who considered it her due. After a few months of this, Gertrude decided that she would keep 50 cents for herself, which Mom saw as outrageous rebellion. "All these years, I have paid for taking care of you and provided everything you needed," she said.

This was the same way she dealt with our older brothers, Bud and John, who worked in the factory and handed their whole pay over to her, except for a small allowance for tobacco and other needs. But Gertrude stood firm, and Mom finally yielded. At 19, after working in the factory (which had just begun hiring young women) herself, she found employment with a young physician. His first marriage had ended in divorce, and his second wife was a young nurse who had grown up in the Upper Peninsula of Michigan and was very insecure about her roles as a wife and the mother of two small children. Knowing of my sister's sterling reputation for caring for small children and keeping house, they hired her at a salary that was twice what she could have earned in the factory and much more than other young black women in Albion were making as domestic workers. Their children became deeply attached to Gertrude and were inconsolable when she was not there on weekends. This physician eventually left the practice of general medicine because of the extreme distress he felt whenever one of his patients died, and trained as a psychiatrist in another state, where he practiced until he died in 1972. This family, including the children, still keeps in touch with my sister. Gertrude eventually married twice more and had two children of her own, both of whom went on to have professional careers. Like our mother, she ultimately became a landlord, owning three homes and achieving financial security.

My early years in Albion provide some important insights into the success of American black communities from the 1920s through the 1940s. They show what results when black men have jobs that pay a good salary: marriage, home ownership, children who perform well in school (even if it is inadequate and unequal), community churches which are well attended, and social clubs and groups that cut across religious lines. My friends and I cannot recall an instance in which a single mother was raising a child alone. If a girl became pregnant and did not get married, the extended family members improvised a way of disguising who fathered the child; in any case, the girl and her baby lived within the family clan, who cared for them.

The stigma of out-of-wedlock pregnancy was forceful and effective. To illustrate: One young man who impregnated a girl was the first member of the black community to attend Albion College. He and his family did not want him to marry her because of her dark complexion and lower social status. When the girl's father threatened to kill him, that ended his college career; he moved to Chicago, never to return to Albion. Even if an expectant couple decided to marry, they wouldn't be allowed to have the ceremony in any of the three black churches. The mom-to-be and her husband often were required to stand before the congregation and ask forgiveness. (A similarly high standard of conduct was required of ministers in the Baptist churches, who were forced to resign if two-thirds of the members supported the board of deacons in removing them; if such a majority could not be obtained, the congregation would be split and another church formed. The misconduct that could lead to dismissal included such behaviors as financial corruption, sexual promiscuity, and marital infidelity.)

As for black-on-black crime, my friends and I could recall only four homicides from the 1920s to 1950, through years of prosperity, depression, and war; and all were related to disputes about sexual partners. Also (on an altogether different matter) none of the children of the five black families in Albion who were most successful in operating small businesses went to college in the decades under review. For each of those families, making money held greater prestige than educational achievement.

Nonetheless, when a black student succeeded in college, the entire black community held that student in high regard, as certainly was true in my case and with my few peers. The most dramatic achievements by far occurred during the 1920s, prior to the Great Depression; the first wave of the Great Migration of blacks, starting in 1915, created a group of ambitious people who had high hopes of finding a better way of life for their families.

FIGURE 1-1. My mother and father's wedding picture in 1920. This is the only known picture of my father. He was a leader in the Albion black community and head of the black Masonic Lodge. The black American Legion chapter was also named for him. My mother managed the family finances and tried to manage my father.

FIGURE 1-2. Me (right) at age 2 and my younger brother Tom
at age 6 months.

FIGURE 1-3. Me at age 4 in a sailor suit bought by my oldest sister Lucille.

FIGURE 1-4. A classroom in Austin School, which I attended
from kindergarten through grade 6.

FIGURE 1-5. A classroom in the black elementary grade school attended by
my two younger brothers and youngest sister Gertrude. The black teacher is Ruth
Ferguson. In later years I was a close friend of her and her husband Clifton.

FIGURE 1-6. In front of our home at 1011 N Albion St when I
am about 7, my brother Tom age 5 and brother Uly age 3, and our
nephew Charles, the oldest of Lucille's children.

FIGURE 1-7. Me, Tom, and baby sister Gertrude
in front of our father's Model T Ford.

FIGURE 1-8. Me, Tom, Uly, and Gertrude a few months after our father's death. Our Mom had us shabbily dressed in order to keep relatives in Georgia from begging for some of the insurance money which came to her after he died and which she used to upgrade our home to provide indoor plumbing, electricity, and furnace heating.

FIGURE 1-9. My second older brother John in his early 20s and an important early role model for me. He was blacklisted and refused further employment for attempting to organize a labor union in the leading local factory. He is pictured here with Mattie Howard, a black teacher in the black elementary school. John left Albion and spent the rest of his life in Detroit.

Debate

This year the debate squad, the orator, the declaimer, and the extempore speaker brought the Twin Valley speech cup to our school. They also brought numerous state awards for which we are very proud.

The squad, under the coaching of Mr. Cobb, entered the state eliminations with only one veteran debater. The others, however, proved themselves true debaters when they won three debates in state finals and were defeated when there were only eight schools left in the competition.

We congratulate these debaters and sincerely hope that they can bring a State Championship to our school next year.

The members of this year's squad are: Seated: Herbert Fredenburg, Jeanette Barcroft, Dorothy Hall, Virginia O'Dell, Virginia Carter, Pauline Grenier, Marilyn Harger, Helene Jarvis, Edward Neil. Standing: Eugene Wilkinson, James Curtis, John Randall, Mr. Cobb, Jack Kellogg, Wendell Allen, Phil Baldwin.

FIGURE 1-10. A yearbook page of the high school Debating Squad of 1940.

JAMES CURTIS—"An earnest, straight-forward man." Honor Society, Honor Roll, Student Council, Breeze Staff, Extemporaneous Speaking, Debating.

DOROTHY BUSHINSKI—"You cannot do so much in the short span of life." BARBARA BUSHONG—"Mirth and motion prolong life." Thespian Club, Thespian Play, "A" Club, Executive Board, Junior Ex., Breeze Staff. BETTY BUTLER—"Her air, her manner, all who saw admired." Business Club, "A" Club, Office Practice.

CHESTER BUTLER—"Every man is the maker of his own fortune." Track, Golden Gloves. ORPHA CARBAUGH—"The harmony of life is my goal." Basketball, "A" Club, Band, Exchange Assembly, Ushers' Club. JESSIE CARNELL—"The more we do the more we think we can do." Honor Roll, Choir, Junior Ex., Library Staff, Camera Club.

DONNA JEAN CASE—"Talent is something but tact is everything." "A" Club, Junior Ex., Office Practice, Exchange Assembly. JAMES CURTIS—"An earnest, straightforward man." Honor Society, Honor Roll, Student Council, Breeze Staff, Extemporaneous Speaking, Debating. HELEN DeFOREST—"Not by years but by disposition is wisdom acquired." Business Club, Office Practice.

MARIE DeFOREST—"Who deserves well, needs no other's praise." Student Council. LEO DeMETRICK—"A good disposition is more to be desired than gold." Basketball, Class Softball, Athletic Board, Track, Safety Control Club. JAMES DeMAGGIO—"Good humor is the sunshine of the world." Football, Class Basketball.

CARSBY DIXON—"Worry and I have never met." Baseball, Football, Basketball, Band, Track. LOUISE DODES —"An air of quiet unaffected assurance." Concord High, Choir, Band, Office Practice. ROY DODES—"He who serves well and says nothing makes claim enough." Class Softball, Class Basketball, Track.

WILLIAM DOPP—"No one knows what he can do until he tries." Junior Ex., Class Softball, Class Basketball. DOROTHY DOTY—"Cheerful, good-natured, always smiling." Exchange Assembly, Basketball, Choir, "A" Club, Business Club, Junior Ex. KATHERINE EGMER—"Truth is the highest thing that man may keep." Niles High School—Typing Club, Choir.

FIGURE 1-11. My graduation picture from the yearbook. I was voted by my classmates as "most likely to succeed."

FIGURE 1-12. William Beck (center), a Sunday School Superintendent at Macedonia Baptist Church and an important role model. My father and older brothers never attended church. My mother and all my sisters were devout Baptists and church leaders.

FIGURE 1-13. "Doc" Anderson, Scoutmaster of the black troop to which I belonged until I finished high school and an important role model.

CHAPTER 2

Albion College and the University of Michigan, 1940–1946

Y THE TIME I entered Albion College, I was increasingly looked upon as a spokesman for the local black community, and I recruited several of my professors to become NAACP members when I was a freshman. Thanks to the unspoken but powerful separation between "town and gown" at that time, only Carol Lahmon, my speech professor, regularly attended meetings. Many local organizations invited me to speak on inter-racial affairs. Our NAACP chapter brought a lawsuit against a restaurant that refused to serve Doc Anderson, my former scoutmaster; the restaurant owner filed for bankruptcy and closed his business before the trial could begin. Mr. VanDellan, the young lawyer who was my mentor at the time, was to be our lawyer in that trial.

But I wasn't all business. I enjoyed socializing with others of my age, partic-ipating in parties and dances, going out with girls, and learning—and teach-ing others to play—bridge and chess. I had been seriously involved in music since my junior high years, and was president of the glee club for two years in high school. In my senior year of high school, I was given the opportunity to take voice lessons from Mrs. Darleen Miller who, along with Miss Nema Phipps, operated a private academy that provided instruction in voice and piano. Mrs. Miller had heard me sing and believed I had talent; she offered to let me work as her gardener to pay for my lessons. I learned a lot about both vocal music and gardening over the next four years, and performed in a number of public recitals, both solo and with other students. I had also played piano for several years at my church, first for the Sunday school and later for the church choir, and also was head of the local Black Baptist Young People's Union. I found it increasingly difficult, however, to subscribe to the fundamentalist beliefs of the church.

My oratorical skills continued to serve me well in college. As a freshman, I received a gold medal for placing first in the men's section at the State Inter-collegiate Extempore competition for a speech entitled "Should the United States Cooperate with Great Britain to Preserve the Independence of China?," and also won the Albion College annual Senior Horn interclass oratorical contest. I repeated this victory two years later with an oration called "Let Freedom Ring." Also in my junior year, I was inducted into Delta Sigma Rho, the national forensic honor society, and captured second place (I should have been first, as we shall see) at the society's Midwest regional competition at the University of Wisconsin in 1942.

When the United States entered World War II following the Japanese sur-prise attack on Pearl Harbor, black Americans were still seen as members of an inferior caste unfit for combat. They were welcome in the military only in unskilled work battalions, just as they had been in World War I—and even back to the beginning of the Civil War. A 1940 War Department memo-randum to President Roosevelt explained that a racially segregated military was necessary because "the policy has been proved satisfactory over a long period of years, and to make changes now would be destructive to morale and detrimental to the preparation for national defense." The War Department went on to explain that combat was not a suitable role for blacks, and that they should be commanded by white officers because blacks could neither fight nor lead; they were "careless, shiftless, irresponsible, immoral, untruth-ful" but, on the other hand, also "cheerful and uncomplaining if reasonably well fed."

On the civilian side, American industry was gearing up to meet the manu-facturing needs of the war effort, but the ensuing rise in the demand for work-ers did not include blacks, who were deemed unsuitable for these high-paying defense jobs. The black press and a newly assertive civil rights movement, led by A. Philip Randolph, president of the Brotherhood of Sleeping Car Por-ters, and Bayard Rustin, his young assistant, threatened to organize a march on Washington to demonstrate to the world that blacks in America were not enjoying the freedom we were trying to spread abroad. The prospect of such a demonstration caused President Roosevelt to issue an executive order opening up jobs in the defense industry for blacks.

Meanwhile, I was competing in the Midwest regional competition of Delta Sigma Rho's annual contest for the national championship, held that year at the University of Wisconsin in Madison, and felt it was important to face these issues. (See the appendix for the text of the speech.) The oration was a huge success, and my Albion teammates and I returned to the dorm where we were housed in time to hear the university radio station announce that I had won. The thrill was short-lived, however; 15 minutes later, the station announced that the judges had made an error and that I had actually placed second to a student from Northwestern University.

Professor Lahmon immediately uncovered what had happened. Four of the five judges had given me a 5, the top score on the scale; the other judge rated me a 1. The other judges concluded that he had inadvertently given me the lowest, rather than the highest, rating, but further discussion confirmed that he was in earnest. Professor Lahmon arranged for me to meet with this judge, who assured me that while he was sorry if my feelings had been hurt, he had given me what he thought was an honest score. I soon realized that my speech could, indeed, have rankled someone holding the traditional view that black people should be content to know and accept their place and make the best of it. I also remembered that when I had earlier given the same speech for a student audience at Albion College, Professor Lahmon told me that one of the students, whose father was a U.S. Navy officer, had said he felt like attacking me and was promptly reprimanded and warned of the serious consequences such an action would bring. Even now, as I read the words of this oration, I can see how clearly my mission in life had already been set, and that it would never be a lack of courage that moved me off course, nor even my awareness that I had not only enemies but also many friends of all races and creeds.

At Albion, I was a close friend of several of the small number of Jewish students, of another student who was of Arab origin, and of two Japanese students who, along with their families, had been sent to a concentration camp in California out of fear that they would become enemy aliens in our fight against the Japanese (one of the great failures of morality of President Roosevelt and the New Deal). Both of these young men were planning to become engineers and we continued our friendship when they later went to the University of Michigan. One of the Jewish students had a job, as did I, working for the National Youth Administration, which employed college students to help pay their way through school. He and I organized a boys' club at the segregated West Ward Elementary School in Albion for after-school sports activities, trips to various places in town, and hikes in the countryside on some weekends. Years later, after I returned to live in Albion, some of the older men in the community reminded me that they were among the boys who enjoyed being members of that club.

A stirring speaker at College Chapel one Wednesday morning said that the three great evils of our age were nationalism, capitalism, and war. I became convinced that every person alive must make a personal decision to be for or against the unholy trinity. Nationalism should be replaced by one-world citizenship and government, capitalism by democratic socialism as outlined by Norman Thomas, and war by non-violent conflict resolution and mediation as an application of Christian faith and the principle of the Golden Rule, endorsed by all the world's great religions. Thus, when the United States entered World War II and the draft was revived, I came to the conclusion that I could not be a combatant. Becoming a cleric offered an exemption from the draft, but I could not see myself entering the ministry, although my professor of philosophy and psychology, John Marshall, thought that should be my mission in life. In fact, he told me that I was too much under the influence of radical members of the faculty who had limited foresight, and that leaving the Baptist church of my childhood and becoming an Episcopal priest would improve my chances of becoming an effective leader of my people.

That advice came shortly after, and I think because of, a disturbing experience involving other faculty members. My history professor, who was known to be the most politically radical member of the faculty, was married to my Spanish professor. On several occasions, she had asked me to come with her to sing songs in Spanish when she was invited to speak at nearby women's club meetings on topics relating to Spain, where she had lived and studied. One evening, we went to the Albion Women's Club. That very day, I had been called by the mother of a black high school student who contacted me as head of the NAACP to tell me how her daughter had been mistreated in school. When a teacher reprimanded the girl for talking out loud and arguing with another girl, she cursed the teacher, who called the guidance counselor, who called the police, who arrested the girl and took her in handcuffs to the county jail in Marshall, 12 miles away. Only then was the mother contacted, and she went to Marshall, where the authorities released her daughter to her. The mother thought they should not have been submitted to such humiliation, since her daughter had no previous record of behavior problems and the mother was at home and could have been called by phone to come to the school and resolve the matter.

Before I sang my songs that evening, I thought it would be good to help the ladies in that room understand that the whole Albion community should be disturbed by mistreatment of this kind, and let them know that our local branch of the NAACP would be writing to the superintendent of schools to try to prevent such injustices in the future. At the end of the meeting, the president of the club, who happened also to be the wife of the professor of Romance languages at Albion College, said that she would like to speak to me privately. She calmly told me that I should be ashamed of myself for disrupting their meeting with my unsolicited speech, and that when she was growing up in a nearby village, people who behaved like that would have been publicly whipped. I remarked that I was not only proud of what I had said but also glad that even her little village was probably now more civilized. I am certain that her husband suggested that Professor Marshall try to give me corrective counsel.

An incident involving another of my teachers, economics professor Walter Terpenning, made me more keenly aware of the central role racial prejudice would play in my life. One afternoon, he told me that at his church the previous Sunday, a congregant who owned a large apple orchard near town had announced that the crop that year was so bountiful that church members were welcome to come and help themselves to any apples that had fallen to the ground. Professor Terpenning asked if I wanted to come along with him after class the next day, and I said I would like that a lot. So we drove out to the orchard, each of us with a large sack, and got out of the car and began filling them.

The orchard owner ran out and asked what we were doing. Professor Terpenning reminded him of his invitation. The orchard owner said that he did not mean to invite colored people and that the professor could keep his apples, but I would have to empty my sack. I did so, and Professor Terpenning and I returned to his car in silence. On our way back to town, he said that I was welcome to his apples, but I respectfully declined; I felt as if they might as well have been poisoned. He said he regretted putting me through that humiliation, and I assured him I knew it was not his fault. Later, I realized that perhaps he was not sorry that he had shown me how the real social and economic world works. Later still, I was grateful for the possibility that he wanted to open my eyes wider to the road I was traveling on.

Two other professors also tried to show me how much they believed in my future. Carol Lahmon, my speech professor who had become active in the NAACP, told me that if I chose to remain in Albion, members of his family would finance the building of a community center where I could run a variety of service programs for the black community. My sociology professor, Melvin Williams, and I had many discussions on ways to bring pressure on the white community to share more political decision-making in Albion. I was emotionally close to both of them and drew strength from their warmth and support.

At the end of my sophomore year, I decided to switch from a pre-law to a pre-medical course of study. Both my life experiences and my reading had made it clear to me that one was more likely to succeed in the legal profession if one came from a well-connected family and was happy defending the social, economic, and political status quo. If I did go into the law, I knew it would be to advance the cause of the labor movement, but medicine began to appeal to me more. The field seemed to offer opportunities for a young person with professional aspirations, regardless of his social background. And if I had to go into military service, it would allow me to be a noncombatant. Besides, Albion College had a reputation for producing top-notch medical school applicants.

Thanks to an arrangement the college had made with the University of Michigan, a student with the necessary qualifications at the end of the third year could be admitted to its medical school and be granted the bachelor's degree from Albion upon successful completion of the first year there. This also shortened the term of study for the MD degree by a year. Professor A. M. Chickering, head of the biology department and advisor to pre-med students, welcomed me to this program, but I would now have to take advanced biology courses and also attend summer school for chemistry and physics in order to complete the necessary pre-med work by the end of my junior year.

Albion held its summer classes at the Bay View Academy, located just outside Petoskey, Michigan. As at the college, student dormitories there were restricted to whites, so the dean of the summer school arranged for me to board with a black family in Petoskey who lived only a mile or so from the academy. Throughout the nation, North and South, living quarters for college and university students were racially segregated. In my sophomore year at Albion College, three of my colleagues on the debate team tried to get me into the fraternity of which they were all members. When the parents of some of their fraternity brothers complained strenuously to President John Seaton, he called each of us into his office individually and read us the riot act.

After my summer at Bay View, I became an enthusiastic member and secretary of the Biology Club, completely absorbed in my studies in that field as well as in chemistry and physics. Professor Chickering inspired me one evening when he told the members of the club that he himself had grown into his teenage years as a totally uneducated boy in a poor farm family in the northern part of the state. After it came to the attention of several professional men in the nearby village that he was bright but had had no schooling at all, a minister, lawyer, and physician privately tutored him for several years until, at age 20, he was prepared to enter college. At the time he told us this story, Professor Chickering was one of the nation's leading experts on spiders, spending his summers in the rain forests of Costa Rica and Panama. His collection at the college was second only to that of the famed Alexander Petrunkevitch at Yale.

He also helped me develop more common sense and judgment on racial matters. One day I complained to him about a monograph written by a physical anthropologist whose thesis was that the facial musculature of Negroes was more primitive and closer to the apes than that of Caucasians. Even if it were true, Chickering answered, he had a problem knowing why it should trouble me. He pointed out that the human hand and foot more closely resemble the "primitive" pentadactyl limb than do a horse's hoof or the wing of a bird, but this does not make them more advanced creatures than we are. Further, human so-called races are only varieties of one single species, as shown by their ability to mate and produce offspring. Our perceived racial differences produce powerfully divisive theories about superiority and inferiority; it's hard to imagine, he added, how human beings would handle matters if we differed among ourselves as much as the more than 300 breeds of dog.

Shortly after learning that I had been accepted into the University of Michigan Medical School, I was drafted into the U.S. Army and ordered to report at the end of my junior year at Albion. Since I had been accepted to medical school I should have been deferred, but as it turned out I had passed the Army entrance intelligence test with a high score. I was therefore assigned to an all-black Army Specialist Training Program (ASTP) company being formed at Camp Wheeler, Georgia. About 50 of us from all over the United

States were to receive eight weeks of basic infantry training and then a six-month crash course in engineering before being shipped overseas for active duty in that capacity. When one other black recruit and I left Fort Custer, Michigan, we were provided with first-class railroad tickets that gave us sleeping accommodations and dining car privileges until we arrived in Macon, where we were to be picked up and taken to the camp. A curtain was set up behind our table at one end of the dining car to shield us from the view of the white diners. When we crossed the Mason-Dixon Line the next morning, everything changed. We suddenly found that there was no space for us in the Pullman car, or even in the coach section. In order to arrive on schedule, we had to ride in the baggage car. We were on time, but covered from head to toe with soot. It was something less than a triumphal entry.

I had no desire to become an instant engineer and had already been accepted to medical school, so I wrote to Professor Chickering during basic training to explain my plight. He and the dean of the Medical School persuaded some Michigan elected officials to get me transferred at the end of basic training to the ASTP unit at the medical school, just in time to begin classes there in September 1943. I found two big surprises on my arrival. One was that the half dozen of my Albion College pre-med colleagues had not had to go through any such ordeal; their draft boards had simply directed them to report to the Medical School in the fall. The other was that the Army had taken over Victor Vaughn House, the dormitory where all male medical students were housed. During World War II, the Defense Department put all male medical students into either the Army ASTP or the Navy's much smaller V12 program. It had been an unofficial policy at Michigan since shortly after the Civil War to admit one or two black students to the Medical School each year, making it one of the most racially liberal medical schools in the nation. I was the only black in my entering class of 175; there were two black men in each of the classes ahead of me. All of us were in uniform, all of us were in the ASTP and, for the first time ever, blacks were living in the university's men's dormitory for medical students. The other black students were assigned rooms together; I was placed with a white roommate because otherwise I would have had a room to myself. I was made to feel comfortable by all the other men on our floor, and my roommate and I were friends from the first.

Little did we realize that the Army captain, who came from a state in the Deep South, was planning to set a booby trap for us. My roommate was a shy young man from Ohio who was unmistakably effeminate in mannerism and speech, which set him apart from others despite the fact that he was friendly and kind. We both were tidy housekeepers, keeping our room free of clutter and all our clothes neatly in place. We had bunk beds and alternated weeks sleeping above or below. Everything seemed to be going well after the first month, not only between us but also with our neighbors.

All lights were to be out at a fixed time every night, and both of us were usually asleep within a few minutes. At about midnight one night, our door was suddenly unlocked and thrown open, the lights were turned on, and we saw the captain in our room. We were both instantly awake and sitting up in bed, asking what was going on. The captain rather sheepishly explained that he was just checking to see if everything was all right. He turned out the lights, closed the door behind him, and left. We both knew exactly what had happened. He was expecting to find us locked in each other's arms, or in some other compromising position, whereupon we would both immediately face charges of homosexuality and dishonorable discharge from the military, as well as from medical school. The man from the Deep South would have saved the honor of both the nation and humanity and shown the danger of allowing the races to live together in military service or in dormitories, of all places. Surprisingly, residents of the rooms near ours seemed unaware that this test had gone on and we had passed, much to the chagrin of the captain, so we both knew it was best to allow it to have been a non-event.

Unfortunately, my roommate was unable to handle the academic demands of medical school, and flunked out at the end of the first year. In retrospect, this may have been due not only to his having attended a small-town high school, but also to the burden he had to bear because of his presumed sexual orientation. Despite his effeminacy, he never made any sexual overtures either to me or anyone else of whom I was aware.

The next roommate assigned to me came from Detroit, where he had attended one of the city's academically selective high schools and then the University of Michigan for premedical studies. Not only did we get along well, but we roomed together for the duration of our stay in the dormitory while it was under military control.

In order to speed up physician production, medical students attended classes year-round during the war, with only a short break during the holidays. The third year was devoted to clinical work on the university hospital wards, and race came into play for me several times.

On a regular evening visit to one of the patients to whom I had been assigned, a white man from a small upstate farm community, I found him crying as I pulled the curtain around his bed to give us privacy. I asked him what was wrong. He said some of the other men on the ward were teasing him because he had a colored student doctor. I told him to tell them that they should wish they had me on their cases, since I was one of the best students in the class. My bravado put him at ease, and he no longer felt belittled.

A boy of three-and-a-half in the pediatric ward smiled when I examined him and, in a singsong voice, laughingly said to me, "You didn't wash your hands." I said, also in a sing-song voice, "Oh yes, I did wash my hands." When he repeated his playful reprimand, I showed him that, although my hands were brown, his hand stayed clean when I rubbed my hand on it. As we continued with the examination, I could tell that he still had a lingering suspicion that I needed a little soap.—

Students in the obstetrics and gynecology rotation, who spent a month helping deliver babies, were sent to Women's Hospital in Detroit because Ann Arbor's population was too small to provide a sufficient number of cases. But black students on that rotation had to go to one of the three black teaching hospitals in the nation—Harlem Hospital in New York, Homer G. Phillips Hospital in St. Louis, or Provident Hospital in Chicago—because Women's Hospital did not want black students on their wards. I chose to go to Chicago and, while I had a good experience there, it was jarring to be singled out in this way. It must have unsettled some members of the U-M faculty as well, because I was the last black student who had to travel that far for that rotation. The two black men and one black woman in the class behind me remained in Ann Arbor to do their obstetrics rotation at the university hospital, while their classmates went to Women's Hospital. That was done for a short while, but after a few years the University Hospital's much expanded obstetrics and gynecology service and a growing local population made it possible for all students to complete this rotation in Ann Arbor.

When I was in my second year of medical school, the American Red Cross conducted a blood drive for the military. My blood type was Rh O negative, meaning I was a universal donor who could give blood to any of the other types. I went to the blood-drawing station at University Hospital on the appointed day, and was greeted by a technician who had me sit down, take off my shirt, and prepare my arm. Then she asked to be excused for a minute and, on her return, she informed me that because I was colored, I could not give blood. This hit me like a ton of bricks, and telling me she was sorry didn't help matters. I went to my room and wrote a letter to the editor of the *Michigan Daily,* the student newspaper, expressing my anger and humiliation at this assault on my dignity, another example of the routine trampling on the feelings of black people.

The publication of the letter gained me many friends, and introduced me to a wider segment of the student community. I already knew of residence halls where most of the students, like a few of my close friends from Albion College, were inclined toward socialism and belonged to the Fellowship of Reconciliation, an interfaith organization that was pacifist and committed to racial justice. I also became close friends with students from residence halls more oriented toward Communism, as well as a number of black students who lived in small college approved residences for black men and women, and this last group was the center of most of my social life.

Taverns and restaurants in Ann Arbor were still segregated at that time, even though it had been illegal for several years in Michigan, so a group of my liberal friends and I formulated a plan to desegregate one of them. Some of my friends in the Fellowship of Reconciliation took part in an experiment that suggested how to integrate a restaurant: a group of five white students and I go in and sit down at a table. Most likely, we would be served; then, next time, it would be two blacks and four whites, and then half and half. The plan worked, and this was years before lunch counters were desegregated by black college students in the South. In retrospect, I can see that this was easier to do in an integrated student community.

World War II came to a close at the end of my third year in medical school, which meant that we were discharged from the Army. To our surprise, the black medical students were also immediately discharged from the Victor Vaughn House. Learning of this affront, a faculty member told me that he knew a young white couple who had just bought a house a few blocks from the Medical School and University Hospital and would rent their upstairs rooms to me and the two black men in the class just behind me. The husband was a graduate student in architecture, and we all remained friends for many years. My last year of medical school was spent as a civilian, but the G.I. Bill of Rights paid my way.

Our entering class of 175 had shrunk to 145; in those years, inadequate grades were quickly followed by dismissal, with little opportunity for make-up examinations. I placed 28th in the class.

The next hurdle was obtaining an internship. This could have been a matter of some difficulty, since only six major hospitals nationwide accepted black applicants: two in New York and one each in New Jersey, Cleveland, St. Louis, and Chicago. But black physician groups in Detroit had pressured Wayne County General Hospital, just outside that city, to provide internships to blacks, and I was fortunate enough to be one of the first two applicants to be accepted.

Deciding my career direction was no easy matter. While I was drawn to psychiatry and fascinated by the writings of the psychoanalytic authors who were beginning to dominate the field, I was put off by its subjective obscurity and lack of objective data—in other words, its non-scientific cult-like approach. Reading the basic works of Freud was something I did for pleasure, but I was already becoming aware that behavior was motivated not only by unconscious biological drives but also by sociocultural group processes, as described by the faculty of Columbia University's psychoanalytic clinic for training and research. Dr. Viola Bernard, a member of that faculty, was part of a small but influential group dedicated to the admission of black physicians to the fields of psychiatry and psychoanalysis. Meanwhile, financial resources to pursue the expensive course of post-graduate training in psychoanalysis had become available from the National Medical Fellowships, which had just been founded in 1946 by Dr. Franklin C. McLean, a professor at the University of Chicago, to provide scholarships for minority medical students. I was able to meet personally with both Dr. Bernard and Dr. McLean, who encouraged me to pursue post-graduate study in psychiatry and psychoanalysis on completing my internship training.

CURTIS, JAMES
Albion

Omicron Delta Kappa
Biology Club
Boys' Club

Seniors

CURTIS, HELEN
Detroit

Alpha Chi Omega, Treasurer
Contributors' Club, Secretary-
Treasurer
WAA Board
YWCA

CURTIS, JAMES
Albion

Omicron Delta Kappa
Biology Club
Boys' Club

DALES, ROBERT
Monroe

Tau Kappa Epsilon, Senior
Class President; Forum Club,
Vice-President; Spanish Club;
Interfraternity Council; A Club;
Football, Varsity; Track, Var-
sity

DAVIS, ELIZABETH A.
Detroit

Delta Gamma, President
Mortar Board
Kappa Mu Epsilon, Secretary-
Treasurer
WSGA, Treasurer
Zeta Epsilon Lambda
WAA
YWCA

DE YOUNG, F. WARD
Grand Rapids

Sigma Chi, President
Interfraternity Council

DICKISON, GEORGE
Sault Ste. Marie

Goodrich Club
Chemistry Club

DUGUID, S. BENJAMIN
Northville

Delta Sigma Phi
A Club
Football, Varsity
Basketball, Varsity

FOBERT, MARGARET
Liberty, New York

FORD, ROBERT
Grand Blanc

Delta Sigma Phi
A Club
Basketball, Varsity
Navy Club
YMCA

FRANKS, MARJORIE
Mt. Pleasant

Delta Zeta
YWCA

GABLE, GORDON
Ypsilanti

Tau Kappa Epsilon, Vice-
President
Delta Sigma Rho
Forum Club
Debate
Publications Council, President

GIBB, ALICE
Midland

Zeta Tau Alpha
Kappa Mu Epsilon
WAA

FIGURE 2-1. My Albion College graduation photo.

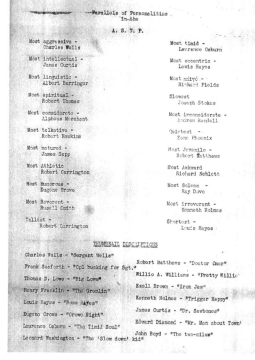

FIGURE 2-2. The Black Infantry Basic Training Company for black members of the Army Specialist Training Program (ASTP) recruited students from black high schools and colleges and trained as engineers to build roads and bridges for WWII troops abroad. In September 1943 I was released from that Company and allowed to come to the ASTP Unit at the University of Michigan Medical School.

FIGURE 2-3. Between 1943 and 1946, while I attended Medical
School, my family and I became members of the black middle
class. My mother acquired several real estate properties and rented
them to black families coming to Albion to work in factories as
part of the second wave of black migration North that occurred
at the end of WWII.

FIGURE 2-4. My oldest sister Lucille
in this time period.

FIGURE 2-5. My brother Tom's graduation
photo from high school. Shortly thereafter he was
drafted and served in the Army.

FIGURE 2-6. My brother Ulysses after his Navy service. Both Tom and Uly received athletic scholarships to attend Florida A&M, a black college famous for its sports teams. After graduating he was recruited to play professional football by the Toronto Argonauts and led the team to two national championships.

FIGURE 2-7. This photo is from 1942 on one of my visits home from medical school. I am here with my older sister Mary, first woman in our family to drive a car.

FIGURE 2-8. My youngest sister, Gertrude, in 1942.

CHAPTER 3

Becoming a Psychiatrist My Way, 1946–1968

A S THE BLACK POPULATION of Detroit became increasingly powerful financially and politically in the late 1940s, Wayne County General Hospital was forced to desegregate, and began admitting black post-graduate medical trainees and hiring black nurses and other health care professionals. Wayne County General was a 5,000-bed acute- and chronic-care hospital located just west of Detroit, one of the main teaching hospitals for Wayne State University, and a site where investigators from the University of Michigan also conducted clinical research. I was one of the first two black interns there when I began my year of general rotations in medical and surgical services after graduating from the University of Michigan Medical School in December 1946.

The other black intern had graduated from Meharry Medical College in Nashville, one of the country's two black medical schools. His home town was Pontiac, Michigan, where his father practiced medicine; one of his uncles was an attorney who lived in Detroit and was treasurer of the Wayne County Democratic Party. Our year as interns passed without incident. All the staff members at all levels were white except for one newly hired black nurse on a medical ward. Blacks made up only two to three percent of the patient population, despite the large proportion of blacks in Detroit. There were no black physicians on staff, but there was one black internist on the visiting attending staff who came once a week, along with the prominent white physician who had arranged his appointment. It was through my developing friendship with that one visiting black physician that I was introduced to the large black physician community in Detroit.

49

I had become friends with several black medical students attending Wayne State when I was in college and medical school. One of them was Dr. Garnet Ice, who had been part of a group of Army doctors assigned to receive brief training in psychiatry before going overseas to serve the mental health care needs of the troops, much as the Army would have trained me in engineering. They did part of their training at Camp Upton in New York, where one of the instructors was Dr. Viola Bernard, the Columbia University faculty member who was working, along with several other American psychiatrists, to increase the number of blacks in the specialty. She thought Dr. Ice would be a good candidate, but he explained to her that his first interest was in surgery, not psychiatry. Dr. Bernard told him that if he encountered a young black physician who wanted to become a psychiatrist, she would like to meet him or her personally and help provide assistance in getting the necessary training.

So it was that Dr. Ice gave me Dr. Bernard's name and address, and I met her in New York City in 1947, during my general internship at Wayne County General. She told me that Dr. Howard Potter, head of the psychiatry department at the Long Island College of Medicine (which was just about to become the State University of New York Downstate Medical Center in Brooklyn), was recruiting blacks for his residency program there. That program was sponsored by the Veterans Administration; both Dr. Potter and Dr. William Menninger, the director of the Psychiatry Consultants Division in the U.S. Army's Surgeon General's office, were also members of that group of American psychiatrists eager to desegregate the field. Dr. Bernard also advised me that I should apply to the National Medical Fellowships, which was formed to bring more black physicians into academic medical careers, to finance the personal psychoanalysis required to enter that subspecialty. I applied to, and was accepted by both within weeks. Dr. Bernard also recommended that I apply to Columbia's Psychoanalytic Clinic for Training and Research, so I could pursue some parts of my psychoanalytic training while completing my residency in general psychiatry. I had already completed the first few months of my psychiatry residency at Wayne County General and completed that year before transferring to the State University of New York residency training program.

The residency training program at Wayne County General was directed by Dr. Milton H. Erickson, one of the most creative American psychiatrists of the 20th century. He is known primarily for the application of hypnosis to the field of psychotherapy, and also made seminal contributions to the development of the short-term psychotherapy that has almost eclipsed the long-term treatment which was dominant in this country after World War II. Born into a farm family in Wisconsin, Erickson contracted polio at age 17. The disease almost killed him, and left him comatose for days, after which he was unable to talk or walk. However, through a remarkable feat of self-mastery, and what he later recognized as a self-induced hypnotic trance, he learned to walk again by going alone on a 1,000-mile canoe trip down the Mississippi River, with only $2.32 for food and other supplies. Despite his physical handicaps, his remarkable ability to negotiate with people along the way for food and physical help enabled him to complete the voyage successfully. He was able to walk with a cane by the time he returned, and went on to the University of Wisconsin, where he earned both a master's degree in psychology and his MD in the same year. Only years later did I learn of these amazing experiences in his early years. He never spoke of them to me, nor did he ever ask me a single question about my own formative years. Against all prevailing dogma, he did not believe psychotherapy required any such information; even now his belief would almost seem heretical. Psychiatric training with him was very much like a psychotherapeutic experience.

The Wayne County residency in psychiatry was a three-year program that accepted only two applicants a year. The other first year resident in 1948 was one of my white U-M classmates. We barely knew each other, as he had been a member of the Navy V 12 group in medical school and those men lived in a fraternity house that had been turned over to them rather than in the medical school men's dormitory. He had wanted to be a neurosurgeon but was not accepted into a training program and decided to go into psychiatry instead, much to the displeasure of his physician father, who was a surgeon in northern Michigan. We stayed on the same dormitory floor for psychiatry residents at Wayne County General and became close friends, partly due to a shared interest in classical music. One of his other hobbies was archery, and he tried to help me become proficient in that difficult sport. That never happened, but I was left with a lasting admiration of the intelligence and survival genius that enabled early mankind to survive by their hunting skills. I also enjoyed a friendship with the other black intern and we spent a lot of time learning to ride horseback at a nearby stable and riding school. This was another humbling learning experience. He often went to his parents' home in Pontiac on weekends, and spent a lot of time alone in his room during the week as he was basically a shy person.

Dr. Erickson was pleased with my future plans for training in psychiatry and psychoanalysis and my interest in a career in academic medicine. While he was not a psychoanalyst, he had great respect for some of Freud's contributions and had co-authored several papers with Dr. Lawrence Kubie, a leading psychoanalyst in New York City, who had referred several patients with intractable symptoms to work with Dr. Erickson. Erickson demonstrated how patients, while in a hypnotic trance, used all of the defense mechanisms described by Freud. Most of the attending psychiatrists at Wayne County General were either undergoing personal analysis or had completed it, but the Detroit Psychoanalytic Society, led by Dr. Richard Sterba, was known to be orthodox Freudian and unsympathetic to other views, which did not appeal to me.

Wayne County General's psychiatric division, which was separate from the general medical and surgical acute and chronic services, was a good example of a large psychiatric hospital of its day. The acute care division of about a hundred beds took care of newly admitted psychotic patients; a much larger chronic care division provided custodial care to several thousand more. This psychiatric division was a self-sustaining therapeutic village in every way, with a large farm and grounds and numerous buildings, all maintained by patients who worked under the supervision of paid staff. These patients were not only employed without pay to work on the farm, but also in the power plant, laundry, kitchen, and post office. In addition, they worked in teams maintaining the grounds and roads, and constituted the housekeeping staff. Most psychiatric staff physicians and their families lived on the grounds in houses provided by hospital administration, and were provided with stabilized chronically ill patients to serve as maids, cooks, housekeepers and gardeners to meet their household needs.

Most of our residency training took place in the acute care units, where we were responsible for the initial medical and psychiatric workup of new patients and followed their treatment course thereafter. We learned the treatment modalities of the day: electro-convulsive therapy, insulin coma treatment, and malaria treatment for patients suffering from tertiary syphilis, of which there were many. Patients also received recreational and occupational therapy as well as music therapy, which was a special interest of one of the attending psychiatrists. Some of the patients were professionally trained musicians, who were joined by other musicians in the Detroit area for an annual symphonic performance attended by a large audience. Mrs. Mary Manly, the only black member of the psychiatric hospital's professional staff, was chief of the music therapy program.

In the course of working up and following the patients' general course, we residents interviewed family members and worked closely not only with nurses but also clinical psychologists and psychiatric social workers to arrive at our diagnosis and treatment plan. Dr. Erickson, who believed in bedside teaching, would accompany us on our daily rounds, along with the attending psychiatrist in charge of that unit. Outside lecturers came to the hospital once a week to teach the residents various developments in psychiatry, as well as psychology and sociology. Dr. Erickson also believed strongly in the interdisciplinary team. He chaired the weekly journal club, where staff members from these related fields presented articles from their own leading journals. Attendees at these meetings were all professionals: psychiatric staff physicians, residents in training, psychiatric nurses, psychologists, and social workers, as well as students doing field placements in all the supporting professional disciplines. It was at one of these meetings that I met my future wife, Vivian Rawls, who was one of the hospital's first two black social work students, both from the University of Michigan School of Social Work, assigned to do their field work at Wayne County General.

Wherever possible, our training took place in the real world. Dr. Erickson arranged for residents to go to the Detroit Family Court one afternoon a week to do psychiatric evaluations of children coming before the Juvenile Court division for delinquent behavior, or who were being evaluated for removal from their homes because of parental abuse or neglect. And when he was called on for private evening consultations by psychiatrists in Detroit who wanted his help with patients showing little progress, he brought his residents with him to their offices to observe his work with patients directly. Discussions following these sessions became social events that nurtured warm feelings of friendship.

Dr. Erickson's reading assignments for the residents were both unusual and mysterious. He asked us all to borrow the following books from the department's library: *The Golden Bough,* by Sir James George Frazer, the classic comparative study of mythology and religion around the world; *Barbary Coast,* by Henry Asbury, a history of the breakdown of social and personal behavior norms during the California gold rush, and *The Crowd,* by Gustave Le Bon, a pioneering social psychological analysis of crowd and mob behavior. What made these reading assignments a mystery was that Erickson had absolutely nothing further to say about these books after assigning them to us. He never asked if we had read them, much less did we discuss what he or we thought about them. This was an example of Dr. Erickson's therapeutic strategy; he was forcing us to make our own individual interpretation of how to handle the assignment. Each resident was left to deal with his private decision about how he chose to act. He had to decide for himself whether to read these assignments or not, or to wonder how he might discuss the subject matter at some future time. This taught us to accept personal responsibility for our choice to be an excellent, good, average, or below-average professional person without anybody checking up on us. In this way, we learned that in the privacy of our own thoughts we are not only tested but also grade ourselves.

After leaving Wayne County in 1968 to move to Phoenix, Dr. Erickson gained a worldwide reputation for his great and original genius, as both a teacher and therapist. He would often assign patients to climb a nearby mountain, and leave them to search on their own for the meaning of accomplishing that particular task, why he had given it to them, and its relevance to their illness. Hundreds, even thousands, of possible ideas would occur to patients, in the course of which their symptoms often would abate as mysteriously as they may have developed in the first place. This is teaching by metaphor.

Dr. Erickson resisted calls for him to develop a school of thought on human behavior, insisting that he be considered atheoretical. He believed that each person's unconscious mind has individually created its own theory of why he behaves in his or her personal way and that his or her unconscious mind can find a better solution for the problem created than anyone else can, including the therapist, if presented with a therapeutic situational challenge. In his view, everyone goes in and out of various stages of trance throughout the day, and it isn't necessary to induce a formal trance state for a patient to be a therapist for himself. Nor did he think it was necessary to explore a person's life history, or to interpret his or her dreams or fantasies or memories of the past. The therapist's task was to do whatever was necessary to create a situation in which the patient can find his own solution to his difficulty. Removal of symptoms was still the aim, but achieving it was not the therapist's job. Erickson was also a great practical joker, who enjoyed using both metaphor and game playing as learning opportunities. He invited me to have dinner with him and his family on several occasions, and I vividly remember the first one, and my introduction to this tactic of his.

1. The Coin Toss Game

Erickson, one of his sons, and I were making small talk in his living room before dinner. He asked if I had any change in my pocket. I said yes, and held out my hand to show the coins. He asked me to hand the quarter to him, which I did, at which time he flipped it and covered it with his hand.

"Heads or tails?" he asked, to which I answered, "I would guess tails."

"It's heads," he said, "I win." He asked if I would hand him another coin and I gave him a nickel. As with the quarter, he flipped it, covered it, and asked if it were heads or tails.

"Let's stop," I said. "There's something wrong with this game. You take a coin which is already mine, flip it, and then give me a chance to win it back?"

He grinned, as did his son.

I said, "It's a peculiar game if you are the only one who can win."

Then we all laughed, and he gave me back the nickel. "I wondered how many coins you would lose before you caught on," he said. I sat there for a moment, pleased with myself, when he asked, "And would you also like to have your quarter back?" Embarrassed that I had not remembered to ask for it myself, I said I surely would.

This experience was both unsettling and funny, as I pondered how gullible I had been. One of his findings was that a slight sense of confusion would enhance trance induction, so my momentary bewilderment showed that I was probably in a light state of trance. I certainly didn't feel hypnotized, but in retrospect I must have been. What did I learn from this prank? That it is one thing to trust a person in authority who is your teacher, but quite another to be gullible and easily exploited. This profound lesson was certainly a good one for a fledgling psychiatrist, or even an old psychiatrist, and it taught me a lot about how to appraise an appropriate doctor-patient relationship or, indeed, any relationship.

Another training director and I were talking a few years later, and he said he would like to share an important lesson with me: there are two kinds of people in life, those who are at least a little bit paranoid, and those who are damned fools. This is a useful aphorism, indeed valuable, but it comes to you like a sledgehammer, while Dr. Erickson's way of teaching was more like a velvet glove. Moreover, he never said a single word to me about what the coin toss game was all about, and for some reason it never dawned on me to ask him directly the why or wherefore of it. All these years later, I'm still coming up with possible meanings and messages from it.

2. The Summer Camp Game

The Rorschach ink blot test presents the viewer with an ambiguous visual object, and his interpretation of what it looks like reveals some of his characteristic ways of finding meaning in the world around him. Dr. Erickson's games were like action scenarios that required a person to act in a certain way, thereby revealing how he might act to manage the world around him and, further, how he might have handled the situation better if given another chance . . . and life itself is an ambiguous situation, a projective psychological test.

At the end of dinner on another evening at his home, he asked if the next day I would do a physical examination and fill out the form for one of his sons, a 10-year-old who was applying to go to summer camp. Of course I would do it, I said. At 11 a.m. the next day, having finished my morning ward duties, I phoned to ask that the boy come to meet me in one of the examining rooms. On examining his chest, I was surprised to hear a loud systolic murmur. I asked if anybody had ever told him he had a heart murmur, and he said yes. Then I asked if he had gone to summer camp the year before, and again he said yes. I decided I should talk about this with his dad and not involve the boy in further conversation. The rest of the exam went well, and the two of us then walked to his home, where his father was waiting. Speaking privately with Dr. Erickson, I told him of hearing the murmur, and wondered if he knew of it.

"Oh yes," he said, smiling. "It's nothing serious; last year the cardiologist said there was no reason the boy should not go to summer camp." I breathed a sigh of relief, and then handed back to him the examination form he had asked me to fill out.

"You should have the same cardiologist fill it out again this year," I said, as I did the smiling.

What did I learn from this trap he set for me? That you should trust your judgment, that you should have the courage to make a decision, that you should not assume that you will be given all the facts you should know before being asked to solve a problem, that you should be willing to help and do a favor up to a certain point only and no farther. I was certain Dr. Erickson had my best interests at heart, but I did not feel good about being tested that way;

it seemed more like being tricked. Nonetheless, I felt I had earned a passing grade. Here again, he said nothing to me about what it was meant to teach, or how I did, but left me to deal with it in my own way. He never even said he was teaching anything or that I was learning anything; that was all in my own mind. Teaching of such a high order is truly liberating.

3. The Walking on Ice Game

Dr. Erickson and I were both leaving the building at the same time one winter afternoon.

Sly fox that he was, I am almost certain that he planned it that way. A mixture of freezing rain and sleet had made the walkway to the building for which we were headed, about 30 yards away, quite slippery. He walked with a cane, so I realized at once that we had a challenge. When Dr. Erickson asked me to give him a hand, I held his arm as firmly and steadily as I could as we began to edge along. He soon said, "Stop. You're doing it the wrong way. All you need to do is hold *your* arm and hand steady. Let me do the holding, not you. I know when to hold tighter, and then more loosely, or not at all. You just need to be there with a steady arm." We walked comfortably and easily the rest of the way.

The lesson here was that you alone cannot accurately anticipate or assess what your patient needs. The patient himself can do it better. Your task is to have the courage to believe that the patient will trust his judgment of what is best for him and can treat himself better than you.

Psychiatrists are particularly vulnerable to this fallacy of omniscience, believing that patients who disagree with them are showing "resistance" to true insight, but patients will be directed by their own inner compass. This is why the best salesman is the one who believes "the customer (who, in this case, is the patient) is always right." Dr. Erickson spent 60 seconds ostensibly talking about walking on ice; I spent a great deal of time over the next 60 years thinking of how that was a metaphor for the best way to be a therapist, a parent, a teacher, a friend. The fact that we found ourselves on a slippery walkway that day was a teachable moment for him and a great learning moment for me, staged by a masterful psychiatrist. Life is a slippery walk.

4. The Phenomenal Memory Game

Dr. Erickson would sometimes take all six psychiatry residents on special rounds to one of the large units where chronically ill patients had been re-

ceiving little more than custodial care for many years. Those who had recovered significantly almost always remained at the hospital and were given
work assignments; relatively few returned to their home communities. Many
patients we saw demonstrated unusual symptoms like waxy flexibility, in
which they remained in odd positions or postures like a statue, and would
sometimes allow an arm or leg to be moved into another position, where it
would remain. Other patients had bizarre delusions and hallucinatory experiences or were totally disorganized and regressed. In giving the history of one
such patient, Dr. Erickson displayed a remarkable memory of the minutest
details of the family history, and various treatment modalities that had been
tried with various degrees of success, followed by relapse. At the conclusion
of rounds, as we were returning to our offices or our room, I stopped by the
medical record room and requested that particular patient's record in order
to verify Dr. Erickson's dazzling performance. I was told that the record had
been checked out by another staff member, and I asked to be notified when
it was returned, so I could come and pick it up. When I returned to my office
minutes later, I saw the patient's medical chart lying on my desk. On top of it
was a note from Dr. Erickson: "I thought you would want to check out this
record, so I brought it to you." It took my breath away to think that he had
read my mind like that.

By this time, I had become more intellectually wary and skeptical, particularly in dealings with Dr. Erickson. The lesson here was that he not only
realized this, but apparently welcomed it as a sign that I was no longer easily conned. When extraordinary feats are performed and remarkable claims
made, always question them, no matter who makes them, including prominent teachers and even your director of training. Moreover, if you do not raise
a question, you can be sure one of your more alert colleagues will. Again, we
said nothing to each other about the incident and, again, it remains as clear
to me as the day it occurred.

5. The Game of Being Black

Dr. Erickson never discussed what he thought about race relations, but his
actions demonstrated that he had warm feelings toward me as a person, which
I reciprocated. He not only spent more personal time with me than he did
with the other residents, but also showed his lack of prejudice in other ways.
He was often invited to speak before groups in the Detroit area about hypnosis and to demonstrate hypnotic induction and the trance state. For several

years, one of his special hypnotic subjects was a young black female secretary in Detroit who was able to go into profound depths of trance. On one occasion, he invited me to come with them for a presentation after a luncheon at a women's club in a nearby town. He introduced me as one of his psychiatry residents, and made it clear that I would have no role in the actual demonstration, which went very well. Only later did it occur to me that Dr. Erickson may also have thought having me along that day would give him cover, preventing wagging tongues from spreading tales of his traveling alone with an attractive young black woman.

One afternoon near Christmas during my training year, I noticed that the whole hospital complex was uncommonly quiet. Going to my office, I found a note on my desk from Dr. Erickson that read something like this: "At 4 p.m. go to room 402 and look inside." Somewhat puzzled, I did as suggested, and saw all the staff, including him, laughing and drinking and having a great time at a Christmas party to which I had not been invited. I felt deeply humiliated and betrayed, realizing that I had been treated this way because I was black.

On my way to my room in another building, I wondered why Dr. Erickson wanted to rub my nose in it but, as time passed, I understood his message: Yes, you do have white friends who care for you, but there are many more whites who consider you less than a person, and the ugly fact is that you can expect to be a victim of racial prejudice and discrimination throughout your life.

Nothing can protect you from that social evil, neither your white nor black friends, nor even your black parents and family. It will be up to you to decide how to deal with it. You can allow it to stunt your full growth and development, or you can have it spur you to a creative response of strength and mastery, rather than tearful surrender.

He did me a favor by confronting me with reality. I have known some black people, especially professionals, who have settled into a safe cocoon with a few white friends, turning a blind eye and deaf ear to other black people and the outside world. Other blacks I have known have slammed the door against all white people, shunning even those who would join them in a fight against a whole set of social evils.

Dr. Erickson challenged me to bring out the best within myself: and he was just the right role model for the job: a crippled, tone-deaf, color-blind specialist in a stigmatized field, who had become one of the most productive psychiatrists of his generation. Working with him was one of the great experiences of my life; he truly helped introduce me both to myself and to those around me. And, most especially, he helped me get ready for New York.

My mentor in New York was Dr. Viola W. Bernard, who had paved the way for my acceptance into both the residency program at the State University of New York Downstate Medical Center and as a trainee in the Columbia University College of Physicians and Surgeons' Psychoanalytic Clinic for Training and Research. Her own life was remarkable in many ways.

Born into a wealthy and prominent Jewish family in New York, she dropped out of several colleges before graduating from Cornell University Medical School, one of only four women in her class. She was a towering figure in the history of American psychiatry, not only for her leading role in desegregating post-graduate training in our discipline, but also as one of the founders of Columbia's Psychoanalytic Clinic as well as almost singlehandedly creating the division of Community Psychiatry, a collaboration between the Columbia University Department of Psychiatry and its School of Public Health. She also was one of founders of the Group for the Advancement of Psychiatry, comprising leaders in the profession who wrote a series of monographs on a wide variety of social policy issues in the 1950s and 1960s, including poverty, child welfare reform, racially segregated schools, the end of war, and nuclear disarmament.

She conducted the personal psychoanalysis that was part of my training, which required five sessions a week for three years. I arrived in New York just a few weeks after my marriage, ready to start my residency and psychoanalytic training simultaneously. When I told her of my marriage, Dr. Bernard said this was a problem, because people should not make major life decisions while they're undergoing psychoanalysis. We began work, nonetheless, but I felt stupid and uneasy about having broken one of the cardinal rules from the start.

Vivian and I both believed it was our good fortune to have been thrown together by fate in the same place at the same time; both of us were among the first blacks to train in our respective fields at Wayne County General Hospital. We decided to marry about six months after we met. Vivian had taught music in the Detroit Public Schools for a year following her graduation from West Virginia State University, but she didn't find the job satisfying and was quick to apply, and be accepted, when the University of Michigan School of Social Work began offering scholarships to attract black students into the field. Her earnings as a teacher had enabled her to get an apartment, which she shared with a friend, and to purchase a car, which helped our friendship rapidly develop into a full-time romance. She had grown up in Little Rock, Arkansas, a more completely racially segregated setting than mine, and had had no experience associating with whites, having attended segregated public schools and what was then an all-black college. The University of Michigan School of Social Work was her first experience in racially integrated education, while that was all I had known. Not only was I very close to several white friends, but Vivian and I spent our brief honeymoon at the summer cottage of the family of one of my Albion College friends. Our intellectual backgrounds did not match, either. She had always received high grades, including at the University of Michigan, but had no background in reading the same newspapers, journals and books that had turned me into something of a young radical. It seemed to me she had no opinion about, or even much interest in, most social issues. But the fact that she was very attractive outweighed all of those minor issues, and so I had gone ahead with marriage plans; not without some ambivalence on my part, which she soon put to rest with her good looks and take-charge manner.

My psychoanalysis was a different story. Lying on the couch five times a week, and saying everything that came into my mind, came close to unraveling my marriage, and I soon found myself, for the first time, feeling anxious and afraid, as I had been warned might be the case.

Dr. Potter had exempted me from spending Saturdays during my residency program in the Northport, Long Island, Veterans' Administration Hospital, where the other residents worked with acutely ill patients in the psychiatry unit, because I had already had a year of inpatient psychiatry at Wayne County General. That exemption made it possible for me to begin work at the Columbia Psychoanalytic Clinic, which scheduled heavy course work for beginning students on Tuesdays and Saturdays. The director of the clinic was Dr. Sandor Rado, who had been education director of the New York Psychoanalytic Society from the time that he emigrated from Hungary to escape the Nazi regime. After he left the New York Psychoanalytic Society to protest its rigid dogmatism, he was one of the founders and the director of the Columbia clinic, the first psychoanalytic clinic under university auspices. He was a brilliant psychoanalytic teacher, but absolutely intolerant of any opinion other than his own, which made it painful to listen to him make statements in his lectures to provoke responses which he would then bitterly denounce.

The essence of his theory of human behavior was based on the evolutionary progression of behavior from simple one-cell animals, which are in a resting state of homeostasis until pushed toward a pleasurable stimulus or repelled by a painful one. Higher animals are similarly guided by pleasurable or painful states of emotion. Pleasurable, or what he called "welfare," emotions, such as love, are controlled by the parasympathetic nervous system. In threatening situations, the emergency responses—such as flight, fight, rage and guilt—trigger into action the sympathetic pole of the autonomic nervous system. Those phylogenetically older layers of our central nervous system still function in human beings, but are supplemented by newer portions of the cerebral cortex which give us the ability not only to fight or flee but also to call for the group membership support available to all social animals, and also to use our higher levels of language and other symbolic instrumentalities. This leads to his thesis that neurosis is an expression of human adaptational failure in social, occupational, and sexual function. The core of schizophrenia, for example, is an innate failure of the central nervous system to register or to feel pain and pleasure appropriately, thus leaving the victim without a reliable behavioral compass.

It has been pointed out that while this theory demystifies Freudian psychodynamics, it borrows heavily from Alfred Adler, one of the earliest defectors from Freud, and even from ancient Greek philosophers like Plato and Aristotle, who saw similarities of behavior in all plants and animals.

Dr. Rado's view of human behavioral motivation was an early version of what we now recognize as the field of evolutionary psychology. He believed that psychoanalysts should pay serious attention to scientific studies in animal behavior, along with developments in neurology, neurophysiology, neurochemistry, genetics, clinical psychology, anthropology, and child development. The Psychoanalytic Clinic was housed in the same building as the New York State Psychiatric Institute. As students at the Psychoanalytic Clinic, we took brief courses taught by scientists of the New York State Psychiatric Institute in all those areas, as well as learning the historical sequence of Freud's theory of human behavior. In recent decades, it has become clear that Freudian psychoanalytic theory and practice did not rest on a firm scientific base. Dr. Rado was clear that human behavior and animal behavior were part of the same evolutionary spectrum, and he dogmatically rejected all Freudian terminology and theory. We know now that orthodox Freudian theory resembles a religious cult not supported by the scientific method since its basic tenets are non-falsifiable.

A personal analysis, required of all trainees, is a difficult experience, but it most definitely offers an unusual opportunity to promote one's developmental potential. In the process of learning to free associate, you begin to lose some of your fear of thinking by saying your thoughts out loud. It certainly was liberating for me to have a more complete view of myself. It requires an act of faith to believe that you can have any conceivable thought and it doesn't make you a bad person; that, in fact, being able to think evil can provide some protection against evil behavior. You learn to listen to your continuous inner dialogue during the day as well as understand the inner dramas during sleep that allusively comment on past, future and feared future experiences. Seeing the analyst five times a week in privacy furthers the development of deep transference reactions, some of which so disturbed me that I would shake uncontrollably while lying on the couch.

Among the first hurdles I had to overcome were my fear of and prejudice against whites, and my hostility toward them, which kept me from achieving the intimacy I often desired. For example, when one of my 15 classmates offered me a bite of the apple he was eating one day, I politely declined, with thanks. As my analyst pointed out, I was sending a loud negative message to his strongly positive offer of friendship. That classmate and I did eventually become friends and exchanged visits to each other's homes, as was the case with four other classmates with whom I developed close personal relationships.

My wife was having even more difficulty in handling a new, less segregated world. In our first year, our Columbia classmates had a party which all of us attended. Vivian and I were having a good time singing and dancing together until she told me she wasn't feeling well and asked if we could go home, which we did. When I asked what was wrong, she said she had to leave because her period was beginning. Dr. Bernard pointed out to me that the ladies room would have solved her problem, as my wife must have known, and that the friendly socializing with whites was most likely what disturbed her. This seemed even clearer when Vivian wanted us to decline an invitation given to me by Dr. Potter, my residency training director, that we spend the weekend on Long Island with him and his wife. Dr. Bernard pointed out that this failure to accept friendship could hurt us in many ways. Fortunately, my wife had been hired as a social worker at Kings County Hospital, where many of my residency training sessions were located, and she gradually became comfortably friendly with at least a dozen white social workers and other staff there.

We soon had a large circle of friends, black and white, and we both became more comfortable New Yorkers. Later, my wife also entered personal analysis, which failed with her the first time, but was more successful the second.

As my own analysis proceeded, new insights came to me that only long-term treatment could have provided. For example, my father had died on February 2, Groundhog Day, but I had not sufficiently grieved his loss. Changes in my behavior that recurred annually at that time of the year made it clear from my dreams that I was having serious anniversary depressive and psychosomatic reactions, of which I was totally unaware. Also, I had an unusually strong sibling rivalry with my brother, Tom, whose birthday was October 27, the exact same as my father's, and I realized that in my unconscious mind this proved my father favored him over me. Most of all, however, the major themes of my life revolved around my simultaneous desire for and fear of money, power, and any kind of sex.

I believe it is only possible to come to terms with issues of that magnitude through long-term analysis. However, because therapist and patient are alone and in private for extended periods of time, in a relationship in which the therapist has dominance and control, it is not a safe situation for the vulnerable patients unless practitioners are in comfortable control of their own behavior. As students in an analytic training situation, one has close working relationships with other psychoanalysts who may be supervising the cases of the patients you are treating. Those supervisory sessions are fertile sources for learning, but you can also be given a jolt now and then. One of these faculty members told me that one of my main problems was that I wasn't angry enough, and more than one male faculty member remarked that I should have had a male psychoanalyst rather than a woman as my analyst and I should realize that, after finishing with Dr. Bernard, I would have to do it all over again with a man.

But the greatest blow to my ego came when Abram Kardiner and Lionel Ovesy, faculty members at the clinic, published *The Mark of Oppression: A Psychosocial Study of the American Negro* in 1951. Their basic thesis was that group characteristics are adaptive in nature, not inborn but acquired. Case histories of 25 Negroes, some of them patients at the associated Columbia clinics and others paid subjects, were selected as representative of lower, middle, and upper class Negroes. This small convenience sample provided interview and psychological test data that led the authors to conclude that a specific Negro personality profile exists. In contrast to whites (not even studied comparatively), "The Negro is a more unhappy person . . . he enjoys less, he suffers more . . . The final result is a wretched internal life. This does not mean he is a worse citizen. It merely means that he must be more careful and vigilant, and must exercise controls of which the white man is free. . . . Moreover, it diminishes the total social effectiveness of the personality." Differences between the races, they wrote, reflect themselves primarily in "the self-esteem systems, in the development of affectivity, and in the disposition to aggression, which, in turn, create different patterns of family structure, the relation between the sexes, the social cohesion and the characteristics of Negro religion and folklore and artistic creativity. The major features of the Negro personality emerge from each with remarkable consistency. These include the fear of relatedness, suspicion, mistrust, the enormous problem of control of aggression, the denial mechanism, the tendency to dissipate the tension of a provocative situation by reducing it to something simpler, or to something entirely different. All these maneuvers are in the interest of not meeting reality head on."

Of course, I was furious that this picture of an inferior stereotype was put forth as derived from scientific data. After discussing it at length with my analyst, I requested a personal visit with Dr. Kardiner to give him an idea of what it felt like to hear a black person openly confront him with a contrary opinion of what black people are like, and show how they can present a point of view head on. I asked him how he would react if a study of 25 Jews in New York claimed to have discovered a typical Jewish personality that confirmed a common stereotype. From the historical point of view, I pointed out that white slaveholders embraced a much different stereotype of blacks as happy-go-lucky, fun-loving, sexually uninhibited Uncle Toms and Aunt Jemimas, because that portrait suited their needs. Dr. Kardiner listened to me patiently and said he would think about what I had said. I felt a lot better having given a rebuttal to a teacher who, in effect, was telling me that I was in the wrong field and had no future.

It goes without saying that all blacks are not alike in their personalities and styles of behavior. This is true of any group, but there is also no doubt that sociodemographic opinion studies reveal sharp differences between groups in matters of political and economic market behavior, reflecting their various vested interests. In an article for *The New Republic* of June 10, 2002 entitled "Civilizational Imprisonments," Amartya Sen makes the point that all persons belong to many groups—religious, national, social class, gender, ethnicity, professional, and occupational, among others—but that each person must be free to choose the extent to which such group membership will shape his or her identity, depending on the contextual and situational priorities. Even within groups, however, there are always varying degrees of conflict and harmony, of cooperation and competition with other groups, although there is one basic worldwide civilization which is shared by all humans.

I can think of an experiment which would shed light on the question of whether or not black people are able to be happy. The study could be run at multiple sites by leading research universities nationwide. In cities with large black and white population groups throughout the country, arrange a dinner dance party for 500 persons of each population group on the same Saturday night. An hour after the party is going full blast, have a photographer snap 1,000 pictures of the revelers. Let trained judges, using a happiness scale from 1 to 10, rate the subjects who were photographed. Even before going through the procedure, you know with certainty which group would rate highest for happiness. Similar rating scales could score the apparent amount and volume of conversation, as well as the level of spontaneity shown in dancing. Then follow those groups to church on Sunday morning and check out the range of emotional, verbal, and musical expression. Really, the notion that black people don't have fun, or relate to, or communicate or compete or cooperate with each other, is preposterous!

As I neared the end of my residency and my major coursework at the Psychoanalytic Clinic, I made plans to open an office and go into private practice, treating adults and children. With financing from the William T. Grant Foundation, I completed a year of training in child psychiatry under the aegis of the Jewish Board of Guardians, whose clinics were located in Brooklyn and the Bronx. That agency did not accept black patients, but I was warmly welcomed as a trainee by the director, Herschel Alt, one of the great organizers of mental health services in New York. The previous year, I had worked half-time at the Northside Center for Child Development, a clinic founded in Harlem by the famous black psychologists Kenneth and Mamie Clark, all of whose clients were black children and their parents. These experiences broadened my clinical interest to working with all age and racial groups. A white psychologist on the part-time staff of the Board of Guardians, who had a private practice and was leaving New York, offered to sublet to me her office on Manhattan's Upper East Side, an exclusive neighborhood.

I had furnished the office and was just beginning to accept new patients when the Korean War broke out in the summer of 1950. In 1952, I was notified that since I had served in the Army Specialist Training Program during World War II, and had received most of my medical schooling at Army expense, I would be required to spend two years of military service, as a captain in the Air Force at one of its base hospitals, as a payback. Before completing my psychoanalytic training, I would have to spend two years treating short-term and long-term patients under supervision. Fortunately, a close friend Dr. Elizabeth Davis, a black woman in the class just behind me at Columbia, was willing to accept my furnished office and my sublease obligation. A two-year hiatus in my analytic training was imminent.

In 1950, my wife and I had purchased a three-story brownstone house in Brooklyn, near Eastern Parkway, from a Jewish psychiatrist who was eager to move his family because the neighborhood was "going black." By 1952, I had finished my psychiatry residency and was eligible for board certification. I could complete my analytic training by seeing my patients in the evenings at Columbia and attending Saturday morning seminars there. Faculty at Columbia arranged for me to go to Washington, D.C., and request that I be stationed at Mitchell Air Force Base Hospital in Hempstead, Long Island. The hospital needed a chief for its psychiatry service, and I successfully applied for that position. I could drive 45 minutes from my home to the Air Force base, then drive to Columbia in upper Manhattan after the workday for sessions with my two long-term patients, returning home at about 8:30 p.m. for a late dinner with my wife. One of the other psychiatrists on my staff at the base was also in training at the Psychoanalytic Clinic, and another was a researcher at the New York State Psychiatric Institute. My two years as chief of psychiatry at Mitchell Field were among the best of my training experiences.

President Harry Truman had partially desegregated the military services in 1948, a job completed by President Dwight Eisenhower, and the stigmas of racial caste and second-class citizenship were fading quickly. For example, I was not the only black chief of service at the base hospital. The chief of orthopedic surgery and the chief of pediatrics also were black, while all the other physicians on our staff were white or Asian. It was hard for me to believe this was accidental, rather than a decision by the top brass in the Air Force to send a strong message of racial equality. Black officers and their families had full use of the Officers Club, and all Air Force personnel and their families on the base lived in totally integrated housing. What a far cry from my World War II experience at the segregated Camp Wheeler Army Base near Macon,

Georgia, or in the all-black Army Specialized Training Program unit to which I belonged. Eleanor Roosevelt and others had forged into being the Tuskegee Airmen, whose legendary achievements in air combat belied the myth that blacks were too ignorant to fly a plane. It was, of course, the 1954 Supreme Court decision, *Brown v. Board of Education of Topeka* that outlawed state-sanctioned racial segregation of schools, reversing more than half a century of a legalized racial caste system.

Our psychiatric service consisted of a 20-bed inpatient unit for the acutely ill, and a large outpatient clinic serving enlisted men, officers, and their families. Our staff consisted of three psychiatrists in addition to me, five nurses, three psychologists, and two social workers. Orders to go overseas sent shock waves through every member of the family, wives and children as well as servicemen. I learned the powerful effect that motivation could have on an individual's clinical presentation. Young men with a history of serious psychiatric illness, who had undergone successful treatment and wanted to be trained as pilots, passed every hurdle presented by thorough interviews and batteries of psychological tests. On the other side of the coin, officers and enlisted men desperate to avoid going overseas managed to look like failures, along with their crumbling families. As chief of service, I also learned the significant role played by medical testimony in legal proceedings against enlisted men or officers, since it could be used to determine their competence to stand trial and cooperate in their defense, or whether they bore responsibility for their alleged misconduct. Skillful examination was also required when servicemen were discharged, since determinations of service-connected disability could affect their pension entitlement.

My first article in a medical journal was accepted while I served at Mitchell Field. It appeared in the *United States Armed Forces Medical Journal* for July 1955 and described a convenience sample of 55 expectant fathers who lived on the base with their families. Most striking was the finding that many of the men unconsciously identified with their pregnant spouses, while others showed signs of reawakened and angry sibling rivalry, most disruptively among those men who had received poor care from their own parents, whose behavior they were repeating. The men fell into three groups, according to the severity of their problems.

There were 17 men in Group A, four of whom were black. All of them had come to the psychiatry service, either voluntarily or on referral from sick call or the military authorities, for serious depression. In one case, this involved a suicide attempt that required hospitalization on our inpatient ward. Other causes for referral were anxiety and irritability that interfered with duty, physical symptoms causing psychological distress or, most troubling of all, acts of covert or overt rebelliousness that, in one instance, led to court martial.

The 14 men in Group B, including the only two commissioned officers in the whole sample as well as two blacks, showed milder symptoms than those in Group A. The 24 men in Group C, two of whom were black, had not been treated at the psychiatry service. They were randomly selected from a group of 240 airmen that I had asked to be screened so their incidence of behavioral problems would represent a normal community sample. A set of screening tools had been administered to them, including a brief family history, current parental status and parental expectancy, record of visits to Sick Call in the most recent six months, a check list of current physical and mental health, and three wishes. They were then asked to draw a picture of an imaginary animal and write a brief story in which the animal was doing something.

Requesting such a drawing was part of my mental status examination of all my patients at the time, and all the men in all three groups had been asked to do this because I had seen them all.

The article was well received professionally and earned inclusion in the *Yearbook of Neurology, Psychiatry, and Neurosurgery,* the annual collection of important articles in the field. But it was also featured in *Time* magazine (August 8, 1955), accompanied by a James Thurber cartoon in which one of two older gentlemen seated in lounge chairs at their club, looking dejected and worn, tells the other, "I never really recovered after the birth of my first baby." Requests for reprints came both from this country and abroad, many friends congratulated me, and other friends pointed to possible problems in my methodology. My satisfaction was unbounded.

But professional success during my days at Mitchell Field was intermingled with several painful and tragic experiences, which reappeared with great force at crucial intervals. I believe that how I learned to cope with those personal experiences gave my life story a special depth.

The first occurred when Larry, our first-born, almost died when he was six months old. His temperature hovered near 106 degrees for six days, requiring us to cool his whole body continuously; most of the time he was limp as a rag. Pediatricians at the base hospital could not determine the cause, but suspected a viral infection. I myself had been hospitalized a week earlier with a case of viral pericarditis (the pericardium is the membrane surrounding the heart) that suddenly hit me with symptoms exactly like those of a heart attack (cardiac thrombosis); I thought I was near death. Several others on the base had been hospitalized with exactly the same illness, all of us recovering completely after several days.

There were other problems. Although Larry's development had seemed normal at first, signs of pervasive developmental delay gradually became obvious. He was slow in learning to walk, in learning to play, in toilet training, and especially in learning to talk and smile and socialize with others. He became attached to objects, like a favorite cowboy gun belt, and had uncontrollable tantrums if they were out of his sight or reach.

Despite these signs of autism, we enrolled him in an excellent private school, which provided him with individual tutoring sessions for most of the school day. But by the time he was eight, we were advised to place him in a day school program for developmentally disabled children. A year later, he was accepted at the same facility for full-time care. One of the leading specialists in the study of autistic children followed his clinical course for 15 years and advised Vivian and me on the best way to meet his needs until he became an adult. Vivian took a leave from her social work position at Kings County Hospital, and spent most of the next five years tending to his needs and also to her own long-term analytic treatment. Fortunately, our professional experience had brought both of us into contact with other parents of children with special needs, and this painful experience drew us closer together rather than tearing us apart.

Our second son, Paul, a bright-eyed, outgoing, cheerful, and talented child, was born two years after Larry, in 1955. We could not have managed without the assistance of one of my cousins, a practical nurse who lived in Chicago at the time and worked in a hospital. She was single and accepted our offer for her to come live and work with us, which she did for some years. Her warm and loving care for both of our boys made it possible for Vivian to return to her professional career. Paul was nine years old when we decided to send him to a New England prep school for boys, on the advice of a psychiatrist friend whose son had gone there a few years earlier.

My wife secured a position in the child and adolescent psychiatry division on her return to work. After two years, she became that unit's head social worker, and three years later she was named director of all medical and psychiatric social work for Kings County Hospital, the city's largest municipal hospital. All the social work schools in the New York metropolitan area sent their students to Kings County for their second year of field placement, where they worked under the supervision of her staff, making her one of the most influential regional leaders in the profession.

Meanwhile, Paul continued to excel in his studies and showed promise of becoming a writer. He graduated with double honors in English and philosophy from Amherst College and was accepted for graduate study at Harvard. After two months of work on the philosophy of religions, he had a psychotic break, suffering from bipolar disorder so acute that he required hospitalization. On his recovery a year later, he was accepted into Harvard Law School, but suffered a relapse requiring another hospital stay toward the end of his first year because he had become non-compliant with medication and treatment. He recovered slowly, and never sufficiently for him to be self-supportive. Vivian and I purchased a condominium for him, and he was eventually able to become a broker, buying and selling antiques, which he did until he died of a heart attack at age 52 in 2007.

My wife had been Kings County Hospital's director of social work for more than 20 years when she retired in 1995. Two years later, she began to show signs of Alzheimer's disease. The illness gradually took its ghastly toll, and she spent the last five years of her life in a nursing home before passing away in August 2007. Four months later, our son Paul died. Both of these deaths brought me to depths of grief and sadness that almost destroyed my soul. Our oldest son, Larry, and I are the sole remaining shreds of our immediate family. He has lived for more than 20 years in a small group home in New York with seven other mentally disabled adults, where he has been well cared for and involved in a sheltered work program during the day.

I have chosen to introduce these painful experiences at this point in my narrative, because they deeply affected my private life for the whole period of my professional life. From the early 1950s onward, I suffered great mental anguish, but I also realized my good fortune in being financially able to provide the best care that money could buy. Providing that same opportunity to others became a guiding mission for me, as I came to realize that a selfish preoccupation with my personal misfortunes paled in comparison with the compassion I should feel for the multitude of sufferers in the world who are hopelessly unable to preserve and enjoy their human potential.

At the end of my tour of duty in the Air Force in 1954, I accepted a half-time faculty appointment as assistant professor of psychiatry at the State University of New York Downstate Medical Center in Brooklyn. The position was offered to me by Dr. Howard Potter, who had accepted me into the residency training program there and who was not only head of the department of psychiatry but was also dean of the medical school. As I had by that time become board certified and completed my training at the Columbia Psychoanalytic Clinic, he actually offered me a full-time faculty position with tenure, but at a salary I could not accept because my family responsibilities required that I develop a larger private practice. We agreed I could accept only a half-time appointment. I was to work in a new building, which was being built to house a research program of studies in psychosomatic medicine, headed by Dr. Robert Dickes, an internist who had also been trained in psychiatry and psychoanalysis. I spent mornings there and afternoons and early evenings in my office, which occupied the ground floor of our Brooklyn brownstone.

My plan was to develop an interracial private practice, since I had become an active member of the black medical society in Brooklyn and was a close friend of several black psychiatrists in various stages of training with me, and both my wife and I had an increasing number of white friends who were our colleagues. Slowly but surely, the practice was growing. Another Columbia psychoanalytic graduate was on the Downstate psychiatry faculty, and his office was located in Manhattan. When an internist in Manhattan referred a young woman who lived in Brooklyn and needed psychotherapy to him for treatment, he explained that his hours were filled, but asked her if she would accept a referral to a black psychiatrist who lived not far from her in Brooklyn, that we had trained together and that he knew I was very good. She accepted and saw me for two sessions. When she next saw her internist, she told him that she was seeing me, and that even though my office was in a black neighborhood, it was all right with her. It was not all right with him. He flew into a rage, said she should stop seeing me at once, and angrily assured the young Jewish psychiatrist who had sent her to me that never again would he receive another referral.

My colleague and I discussed the whole episode, and he said that a segregated neighborhood was a serious liability for me. He suggested I move my office to downtown Brooklyn, preferably Brooklyn Heights, where the leading psychiatrists were located. I agreed with him, and also apologized for costing him future referrals. It could be very costly for a white person to be known to other whites as a friend of blacks. Another white colleague who lived in a suburb confided to me that if he and his wife invited me to their home, a committee of their neighbors would descend on them with vitriol, as had happened to one of their friends who had ignored the color barrier.

Getting an office in downtown Brooklyn or the Heights proved to be a daunting task. After showing me several offices, one rental agent told me that the property owner did not feel comfortable renting space to a psychiatrist. He must have had a lapse of memory on seeing me, because there were already psychiatrists in his buildings. Another agent claimed that another physician who had wavered on the matter suddenly changed his mind and wanted it, immediately after he showed it to me. One of my black friends, a psychiatrist who looked white, and I decided to put the matter to a test, which turned out exactly as we expected. That same real estate agent urged her to rent that same office a week later. It didn't matter that racial discrimination was against the law in New York at that time. Indeed, you recall that I had had an office in a superior location in Manhattan that I had to give up when I was called into the Air Force, and my friend who posed as a potential tenant was still subletting it from me! I was finally able to rent an office in a good location in Brooklyn Heights, with views of the Statue of Liberty and Governor's Island, because I found, quite by accident, a rental agent who also managed the real estate properties of one of Brooklyn's huge and prosperous black Baptist churches, including sites in downtown Brooklyn. With a good location and referrals from black as well as white friends, my practice grew and flourished.

Nonetheless, I began to grow increasingly uncomfortable with the thought of spending my career treating a small number of middle- and upper-class private patients, white or black, but they were the only ones who were able to pay or had the verbal and cognitive skills to be suitable patients. This discomfort led to the major decision to become a psychiatric consultant to child and family social agencies in which social workers were the primary therapists. I was the one with whom they and their supervisors would meet for input on psychiatric and psychodynamic factors that might be hindering the child and family functions. Dr. Bernard, my former analyst, was among the psychoanalysts who had spearheaded this collaboration between social work and psychoanalysis. So was Dr. Nathan Ackerman, who was also on the Columbia analytic clinic faculty. They were moving our field toward family therapy and community psychiatry consultation and away from treating only private patients.

My first consultant role was with the Salvation Army Family Service Agency, which had offices in all the boroughs of the city and served a large part of the impoverished black community. Later, I also became psychiatric consultant to the Salvation Army Foster Home Service, the major social service agency for black children requiring foster home placement and for families applying to adopt children. A large network of child and family service agencies had evolved in New York City beginning in the 19th century, when successive waves of immigrant families came to live there. These agencies, like hospitals, were founded and operated along strictly sectarian grounds: Jewish, Catholic, and Protestant. The Jewish and Catholic agencies had continued to strengthen, especially after huge amounts of government funding began to surpass and supplant the contributions of wealthy philanthropists of those faiths.

Meanwhile, the Protestant agencies grew weaker; their middle and upper classes had earlier abandoned the city for the suburbs, leaving behind a working and impoverished Protestant community that became increasingly black and politically powerless. Even when blacks became a strong presence in New York City, black social service agencies were non-existent. The reason, it seemed to me, was that black churches are of many different Protestant denominations with no tradition of united action and relatively little wealth. This was why the Salvation Army, a Protestant organization with excellent professional leadership but no congregation in the usual sense, had become the principal voluntary social service agency for black people in New York. In another effort to make up for the lack of a strong Protestant social service presence, the New York City Department of Welfare had developed its own public social service divisions to provide services for children requiring foster home placement and troubled families, who were soon to become predominantly black. It was for these reasons that I began to do an increasing amount of psychiatric consultation for the Salvation Army, an agency that never has received the recognition and support it deserves.

The New York City Youth Board, in charge of clinical services to combat juvenile delinquency, developed a special project under which child and family agencies would work with a few hundred of the city's most difficult multiproblem families. The Salvation Army Family Service Agency was awarded a contract to work with 30 of these families, and set up a special team of two social workers, one black and one white, and a supervisor named Melly Simon, widely known for her competence and experience, to do it. I was to be the psychiatric consultant who met with the team in my office for three hours, an entire morning, once a week for five years.

Mayor Robert Wagner had a personal interest in the project's success, as did leaders in the social work field, because an improved pattern of service delivery was needed: it was known that only about 6 percent of the city's families were utilizing two-thirds of its social service resources. The mayor himself met each month with social work supervisors from the agencies with contracts. Also present at those meetings were heads of the city human service departments, such as welfare, courts and corrections, public schools, health, and housing. It was believed that only this high-level political leadership could bring about collaboration among those departments to meet these families' needs.

As a part of this plan, an unprecedented amount of data was provided on each multi-problem family: for example, the entire school record for each child in the family, all of the criminal records of the parents and children, and the histories of social services provided in the past to all family members. It must be recalled that, in the 1950s, every individual social worker's entire work history was available for review by the agencies where they applied for work, including supervisor evaluations, rebuttals by the social worker, and the results of corrective action. This level of sharing information about clients and therapists had probably never been experienced before, and not until later years was there greater privacy protection. Moreover, as I noted earlier, every psychoanalytic candidate underwent a personal training analysis, involving scrutiny of the details of his or her personal life five times a week for several years, prior to becoming certified. Living in a goldfish bowl was an everyday experience in the therapeutic world of that day. Any candidate in psychoanalytic training who self-reported as being homosexual was immediately dismissed from further training, and any reported criminal conduct led to the same end. Only after becoming a certified specialist or a director of a social service did one become immune to this kind of potentially fatal scrutiny. Of course misconduct by those of high authority was almost the order of the day. For example, candidates for psychoanalytic training were immediately dismissed for what was then regarded as misconduct, but certified psychoanalysts who were supervisors led private lives full of scandal, for which they were rarely sanctioned. The same is true of all professionals even now, including priests and heads of corporations.

What our Salvation Army team learned was reported at an annual meeting of the American Orthopsychiatric Association and published in their journal. During our weekly meetings, we heard of the progress being made by these families, all of whom had a complicated network of problems, including physical disability, psychiatric issues, difficulties in school, and how they handled their welfare allowances, their housing, and their encounters with the criminal justice system.

These families could be grouped into four categories. In one were those who cleverly avoided all but the most minimal contact with the authorities. They were unable to avoid it entirely since they were receiving entitlements, and records of their behavior were available to us anyway. Surprisingly, that group tightened up their behavior on their own initiative, as if to justify their position that we should go home and leave them alone. Another group also vigorously resisted our outreach efforts, but they continued to be just as "multiproblem" as before, despite our best efforts. Still another group entered into what seemed to be a good, sustained working relationship, but their insatiable need and willingness to seek help made little or no real difference in reducing their problematic behavior. The last group formed a good working relationship and significantly improved in some areas of family behavior, but they were definitely in the minority and showed few solid gains. It usually took no more than six months for us to determine the category in which a family belonged, and they rarely moved. For example, these 29 families included 67 children ages 6 to 12 years, 28 children ages 13 to 18, and 9 who were 19 or older. In the five years we worked with them, not one of these children received a regular high school diploma. There were 20 school dropouts in the families when we began the project, and another 19 by the time it ended. One-third of the families remained the same overall or were worse off, while the other two-thirds made sporadic temporary improvement, but only in a few areas.

We were criticized mercilessly by one member of the audience at the annual meeting where we reported our findings. A radical who subscribed to the school of thought of the day that all rebellious behavior against authority was praiseworthy, rather than a problem, described our intervention as "soft police work," trying to compel a group of healthy but rebellious families to adhere to middle-class morality. In his view, we were the multiproblem culprits and should be ashamed.

I was grateful for the lessons I learned from years of close work with those families. They were, indeed, in rebellion, but it was an unhealthy and self-defeating form of rebellion and completely outside their conscious control. What I was coming to see was that they needed a healthier and more life-enhancing form of rebellion, and that it would require a whole new set of human service institutions providing help throughout the entire life span. One other lesson, which I learned many years later, is that a therapeutic or other human institution is made more efficient by maximum information transparency, as we had back in the 1950s. This cleansing sunshine, however, was only required of foot soldiers and service recipients, not of the leaders in the social hierarchy. Better law enforcement or policing or privacy protection is no substitute for social institutions that allow parents to care for their families or children to want to learn or accept social behavior norms. Families cannot have responsible and loving parents, able to raise happy and productive children who become successful parents themselves, unless they have good jobs which pay a living wage, a voice in the political rules of the game governing their livelihood and safety, and freedom from exploitation by a privileged elite engaged in perpetual warfare and competitive greed. You cannot oppress the common people by hiring policemen, schoolteachers, social workers, psychiatrists and other therapists to make them happy or send them to prison if they refuse to submit.

When Vivian and I learned that Larry, our first child, had special needs, it prompted us to return to the church, which we had abandoned during our college years. She had been reared in the Methodist church and I was from a family of the Baptist faith. I attended meetings of the Unitarian Church several times while I was at the University of Michigan, and had enjoyed the lack of formality and ritual. I was also drawn to their belief that each person should feel comfortable in creating, based on their own life experience and current understanding, a belief system which helps them accept responsibility to create whatever good or evil exists in our world.

As we were considering which church to join, I became close friends with the Rev. Milton Galamison, pastor of the Siloam Presbyterian Church, one of the oldest, largest and most influential churches in the Bedford-Stuyvesant section of Brooklyn. He received his bachelor's degree from Lincoln University; founded in Pennsylvania in 1854 to educate black men, it was the first degree-granting historically black university in the United States and produced many of the great leaders in the nation's black community. Rev. Galamison went on to earn a master's degree from Princeton Theological Seminary, and was called at age 26 to be the senior pastor at Siloam. The Presbyterian Church had gone beyond its devotional focus of preaching against playing cards, drinking, and dancing, and touting sexual propriety as a gateway to heaven. The denomination's leadership was a more progressive wing, clearly devoted to the Social Gospel of eliminating poverty, capitalist greed, war, and racism. Rev. Galamison was of that more modern persuasion, so we hit it off from the start. He and his wife became among our closest friends and we became enthusiastic members of Siloam.

It greatly disappointed us and the Galamisons that despite *Brown v. Board of Education*, the historic 1954 Supreme Court decision that outlawed racial segregation in public schools, the public school system in New York City, a bastion of liberal thought, remained racially segregated and offered inferior schooling for blacks as well as Puerto Ricans, a growing minority. Even the NAACP was satisfied with incremental progress in changing this situation, leading Galamison to break away and form a new alliance with the Congress for Racial Equality and leftist groups that were demanding more immediate action. Specifically, the city's Board of Education had offered no plan or timetable for change. Reverend Galamison and his supporters staged several massive boycotts of the public schools, in one of which 500,000 children stayed away from classes. But the movement ran into difficulty when a faction began to demand that local school districts should form community school boards, which would completely govern the hiring and firing of teachers and administrators and also control the curriculum. This idea was bitterly opposed by the Teachers' Union and the controversy soon took on an anti-labor and anti-Semitic tone, which Rev. Galamison opposed but could not control. He became a member of the Board of Education (a position which I helped him obtain; as a staff member of the community Mental Health Board I had recommended that Mayor John Lindsey appoint him). After his term expired he essentially retreated from active involvement in what he concluded was a futile mission, leaving him despondent and publicly inactive. The public school situation, as well as neighborhood segregation, remains until this day one of New York City's greatest failures.

During the 1960s, I was a member of the Provident Clinical Society, a group of black physicians and dentists in Bedford-Stuyvesant and a local branch of the National Medical Association, which was formed in the 1890s by black physicians because the American Medical Association refused to accept black members. This was another example of how the black community was forced to become a separate and unequal nation within a nation during that era. It was noted at one of our meetings that four straight years had gone by without a single black student being admitted to the State University of

New York Downstate Medical Center in Brooklyn. As a member of the faculty in the psychiatry department there, I volunteered to chair a committee which would develop a plan to produce black college graduates who were qualified to be admitted. This would require identifying strong students at the junior high school level and providing them with mentoring and other supportive services to assure their graduation from high school and acceptance at a strong college. I made it clear that this was a long-term process, and there was no short cut to seeing it through. Our committee consisted of a woman physician who was a member of the Downstate faculty in internal medicine; three dentists; the president of our local branch, who was a physician and a member of the Downstate dermatology faculty, and me.

The father of one of Vivian's co-workers was Assistant Superintendent of Schools for the Bedford-Stuyvesant community. Her colleague arranged for me to meet with her father to seek his support in helping us find students from junior high schools in his district. He was not only warmly enthusiastic and supportive but introduced me to one of the supervisors of the district's guidance counselors, who helped us assemble our group. Our goal was to recruit 50 seventh graders who showed the potential to become college students six years later. Each student would be assigned to a Provident member as a personal mentor, who would provide friendship and support for the student and his or her family and a $1,000 scholarship upon the student's admission to college. Unfortunately, we could find only 30 members who were willing to have at least weekly contact with a student.

Some members of Provident didn't want to accept only students who scored high on achievement tests and also had a B average or better (as I would have preferred) because they did not think we should leave out youngsters whose grades were not good despite their potential. This is what we decided to do. We also excluded youngsters whose parents had gone to college and were already members of the professional class, again to avoid the appearance of taking only the cream of the crop. We knew that we would need social workers to help us resolve family problems which were hampering a child's progress as well as tutoring for children who weren't performing well, and we found those resources at the local Bedford Mental Health Clinic located in the New York City Public Health building, whose chief social worker and director was in contact with all seven junior high schools' guidance counselors; they kept us informed of the academic performance and needs of their students. We had essential support from the National Scholarship Service and Fund for Negro Students, which provided scholarships for two of our students to attend New England prep schools to groom them for acceptance to prestige colleges, and the Christian Herald Foundation, which provided summer camp experiences for the students.

Our efforts paid off to the extent that, in 1969, we were able to report that 29 of our 30 students had graduated from high school and been accepted to college. Unfortunately, not all of them had the success we had hoped for. One brilliant young man, who planned to major in physics and was accepted at both Columbia and Princeton, went into a panic and dropped out during the summer before he was to begin college, suddenly converting to the Jehovah's Witnesses sect, to which he became fanatically attached. Another became a heroin addict in his freshman year in college and dropped out. The student I mentored personally was biracial, with a Jewish mother whose black husband deserted her shortly after her son was born. She smothered him with affection, which he loathed, and he dropped out during his first year at New York University. Despite his brilliance, his emotional problems probably were too severe for him to overcome and he disappeared from further contact. We knew from the best Board of Education data that, in the same year our students were selected, out of more than 100 high-scoring and high-achieving black seventh graders in Bedford-Stuyvesant schools, fully one-half dropped out before finishing high school. In our group of 30 students, three became dentists, one became a successful hospital administrator in New York City, another became a research assistant for the New York Psychiatric Institute, several went into other fields of teaching and science, and several others went into business administration. None became a physician, but our program was a major achievement.

We learned other things that, although disappointing, were of great significance. Seldom did we succeed in changing a student with poor study habits into one who was diligent. Only about a third of our mentors put serious time and effort into working with their students, and exactly the same proportion of our students seemed ready to accept our support and help, regardless of who was their mentor. As for the students' parents, genuine change was rare. We had to conclude that mentoring programs with the efforts and resources we put into ours have only a limited chance of success, as forecast by this particular one. An article describing the initial stages of this program appeared in the *Journal of the National Medical Association* in 1965.

I decided at this point in my career that I was ready to move beyond being a consultant to individual social agencies, like the Salvation Army, to become embedded within one of the massive public agencies, like the New York City Department of Welfare, which controlled the funding, policies, and procedures of those agencies. My opportunity came on a day in 1965 when I had lunch with a former Albion College classmate who had gone on to Harvard University Medical School and then to graduate work at the Johns Hopkins School of Public Health. Dr. Marvin Perkins had been appointed commissioner of the New York City Community Mental Health Board at the very moment when the community mental health movement was at its peak. Both he and I were convinced that the field of psychiatry had to move from a focus on individual patients to the social institutions shaping their lives. New York City was about to develop community mental health centers in all the city's neighborhoods. These centers were to provide both inpatient and outpatient treatment in order to reduce the need to send patients to state hospitals, where they were receiving mainly custodial and inferior care, permanently isolating them from community reentry. Funding was provided to general hospitals in these neighborhoods so they could add psychiatric departments to their medical and surgical wards and outpatient clinics, to be reimbursed by Medicaid and Medicare funding that was deliberately withheld from state mental hospitals to stunt their growth. The severely mentally ill patients themselves were provided with either Social Security disability pensions, which entitled them to Medicaid and Medicare cards to pay for treatment in these new community-based facilities, or welfare checks. Naturally, there was intense competition among neighborhoods for funds to create these centers, either by building them from the ground up or remodeling or refurbishing existing hospitals, and to hire staff and operate them.

One such center was to be established at St. Joseph Episcopal Hospital, which now found itself in the middle of what had become the almost all-black Bedford-Stuyvesant neighborhood of Brooklyn. Its Jewish director of psychiatry had just told Dr. Perkins of his plan to resign, leaving the position vacant, and none of the other psychiatrists on staff, all of whom were white, wanted to take over. My friend Marvin saw this as a good opportunity for me to realize my new career direction. I applied for the position and, following my interview with the non-physician hospital director and to everybody's surprise (or so it seemed), the psychiatry director suddenly retracted his resignation, to the relief of his professional staff, which was all white except for one social worker. No other psychiatrist at that center had my background of training and certification in psychiatry and in psychoanalysis. The black power elite in Brooklyn, led by ministers with huge congregations, like the Rev. Gardner Taylor, who was pastor of Concord Baptist Church with more than 10,000 members, had a direct line of communication with the liberal Mayor Wagner but did little or nothing to influence him in desegregating public schools, bringing schools in Bedford-Stuyvesant up to par, or equalizing the quality of or improving access to the huge health and mental health services the city owned and operated in the community.

Marvin suggested that perhaps it was for the best, and that if I were willing, he would appoint me to be one of his directors of psychiatry on the staff of the Community Mental Health Board, each of whom had a different area of responsibility. Mine would be to manage the interface between him and the director of the New York City Department of Welfare (soon renamed the Department of Social Services). This meant a reduction in the size of my private practice and income, but I accepted at once because it was a great opportunity. Among my duties were weekly meetings with the director of welfare and his cabinet-level staff who headed the various divisions. I also met weekly with Marvin and my fellow psychiatry directors, who were chief consultants to directors and commissioners in charge of the municipal hospital system, and the departments of health, courts and corrections, education and housing.

I met frequently as well with the heads of the neighborhood-based community health centers and, of even greater importance, with the staff members of the Community Mental Health Board who explicitly represented the interests of Catholic-, Jewish-, and Protestant-affiliated agencies. Nobody was speaking directly for the interests of New York City's black population because things simply were not organized that way, although black persons with influence were sprinkled sparsely throughout the leadership staff of all city agencies.

In my two years in that position, I received an education in how the power structure of the city operated, but as a bureaucrat within that system, I was also able to influence the way it operated, at least slightly. For example, Medicaid reimbursed private practitioners who were qualified as vendors by our Department of Social Services as well as clinic and hospital providers, but the Health Department was responsible for setting standards and licensing. When the director of psychiatry for the Department of Health left the Community Mental Health Board for another position, I took over his area of responsibility as well, and did the same when the director for the Department of Hospitals also left. This meant that my staff of about a dozen part and full-time psychiatrists, as well as psychologists and social workers, and I were the chief consultants for three major human services departments. We were also able to help agencies applying for Medicaid reimbursement eligibility by assuring that their manuals and guidelines on matters such as staffing levels and community advisory board input to their boards of directors met federal standards. This combination of jobs earned me a position of major strength, not only in the city but also with the state commissioners of those respective services and the Governor's Office. My former Albion College alumnus and friend Marvin Perkins had by this time left New York City to assume a position in another state. He was succeeded by a Commissioner who also supported my efforts.

Several agencies became eligible for Medicaid funding with my guidance, such as the Harlem Interfaith Counseling Center in central Harlem, the only voluntary agency providing outpatient clinic treatment in Harlem. I also gained this funding for the League School in Brooklyn, which provided mental health services for children whose pervasive developmental disorders required levels of individualized treatment that regular schools were unable to provide. We also directly assisted in the development of halfway house and alcohol treatment services for homeless men in New York's Bowery, and the establishment of an alcohol inpatient detoxification ward in Harlem Hospital Center.

The opportunity to influence Medicaid funding for the drug treatment agencies in a city plagued at the time by a heroin epidemic was especially exciting. Our visits to both methadone maintenance and drug-free treatment programs convinced my staff and me beyond all doubt that drug-free treatment was effective for fewer than 10 percent of new patients, compared to more than 30 percent of new patients entering methadone maintenance treatment. This work marked the start of a long-term personal friendship and working relationship with Dr. Vincent Dole and Dr. Marie Nyswander of Rockefeller University, who devised that treatment modality, and Dr. Mary Jean Kreek, also of Rockefeller, whose career has been devoted to studies of how methadone maintenance works and its success compared to other treatments.

These sorts of activities convinced me that in order to benefit the greatest number of citizens requiring mental health services, intervention had to zero in on correcting inequities in providing and paying for the care provided by treatment services that, for the most part, had been established by religious denominations primarily for children of their faith. For example, when children had to be removed from their homes and placed in residential treatment facilities, it was not unusual for some religiously affiliated agencies to receive up to 10 times the reimbursement rate of others. These different reimbursements reflect the political affiliation of members of rate setting agencies. Also it is necessary to understand that government funds are usually sent to a catchment area or other locality in such a way as to "match" the services already provided in that area. The State of New York used the same matching strategy in sending money to counties, and the Community Mental Health Board provided statewide federal funds on a matching basis. Medicaid funds went to each state on the basis of an equal match. This meant that states already providing a richer set of services now had to pay only 50 percent of their previous cost with the federal government paying the rest. Thus, states already providing costly services could enhance those services while states that were less well-off received little or no federal funds. In this way, the rich got richer and the poor remained poor. Cities used the same plan to fund programs in different city catchment areas. Government bureaucracies should address the needs of all segments of the populations for the general public interest to be served, which should mean that poor communities get more, rather than less, governmental funding, but that is not the way the system works.

As I mentioned, one of my major responsibilities as the Community Mental Health Board director of psychiatry, working directly with the Social Services Commissioner, was to approve the invoices of providers of mental health services for Medicaid recipients. Some providers submitted invoices for services that would have required more than 24 hours a day to deliver. I decided that certain egregious offenders should be denied further reimbursement, whereupon I was sued for outrageous damages. I was defended by the Social Services Department's legal staff, who often found themselves pitted against lawyers who were also members of the state legislature. Also, several members of my immediate staff of social workers were hired as moonlighters at a therapeutic residential facility owned and operated by one provider. Medicaid was billed for the seemingly incredible amounts of work they performed. Providers knew my social workers had a role in approving vouchers, so they gave them plush jobs and they became plants in my department. I did not allow these staff members to approve vouchers from agencies for which they worked part time.

These troublesome providers were Protestant, Catholic, and Jewish, and more than one was black, making it absolutely transparent that I was an equal opportunity protector of the public interest. President Lyndon Johnson's Great Society initiatives, designed to bring more human services to previously underserved communities, were immediately hijacked by private interests instead. For example, hospital care previously costing $10 a day suddenly cost $100 a day after hospital accountants submitted their figures to show that costs had suddenly gone up. Reimbursement for a visit to a physician, psychiatrist or otherwise, increased from $15 to $25 and still higher. These reimbursement rates were determined by the New York State Department of Health but finalized by the New York State Insurance Board. The Department of Social Services submits the invoices but does not participate in setting reimbursement rates. It is easy to see that hidden control by a chain of state agencies is the hand behind the scenes; it's also easy to see that keeping Medicaid reimbursement rates lower than those for patients receiving Medicare or private care effectively shuts the door to equal access for Medicaid recipients. This escalation of health care costs has continued to be a problem up to the present and is unlikely to be solved until a single-payer system of financing health care is established.

In 1968, I received an offer to join the faculty of the Cornell University Medical College to develop and head a new program dedicated to increasing the number of its minority students, a major policy change for an institution that had seldom admitted blacks. My two years on the New York City Community Mental Health Board had given me an inside view of how the public power system operates. I saw the Cornell offer as an opportunity to become embedded in the system of private power and control and continue my mission to help bring about greater social change in a new arena.

FIGURE 3-1. There are no pictures of my residency training at Wayne County General (1947–1948) or of my time at the State University of NY Downstate Medical Center in Brooklyn, NY, (1949–1953) and the Columbia University Psychoanalytic Training and Research Institute (1949–1954). During these years, I was married to Vivian.

FIGURE 3-2. A view of our St. Albans home in Queens, NY.

FIGURE 3-3. Vivian and me on our honeymoon.

FIGURE 3-4. Our two sons Larry, age 3, and Paul, just learning to walk at age 1. They are accompanied by a friend and neighbor.

FIGURE 3-5. Larry, age 6, and Paul, age 4, on being asked to smile.

FIGURE 3-6. Vivian, Paul, Larry, and me as we go on
our first cruise to the Caribbean.

FIGURE 3-7. Our son, Paul, age 22, graduates from Amherst,
with double honors in English and philosophy.

FIGURE 3-8. Being sworn in by the NYC Commissioner of the
Community Mental Health Board, Marvin Perkins, as Chief Psychiatric
Consultant to the NYC Department of Welfare—both of
us were graduates of Albion College.

FIGURE 3-9. A psychiatric consultation visit conducted by
Dr. Tanner of my staff at the Upper East Side Department of Social
Service Center, whose director, Lillian Zerwick, is shown along with a
mother and son who are being interviewed.

CHAPTER 4

Affirmative Action, 1968–1980

THE TIME WAS RIGHT for change in 1968, especially at Cornell University. Radical black students, dressed in military gear and carrying rifles, had taken over the university president's office on the Ithaca, N.Y. campus, and were demanding increases in the numbers of black students and faculty, a separate residence hall, and the establishment of a black studies program. Cornell's administration was making efforts to comply. However, Cornell Medical College (now Weill Cornell Medicine) is not located in upstate Ithaca, but on the Upper East Side of Manhattan, and was not immediately impacted by these momentous events.

Dr. John Deitrick, the medical school's dean, made a public statement that the medical school would not be admitting black students, on the presumption that they were all unqualified. This put Cornell at a clumsy disadvantage, considering that Harvard had already announced its decision to develop a program to admit more black students, as had Yale, Penn, Johns Hopkins, Stanford, and—in New York City—Columbia, New York University, SUNY Downstate Medical Center, New York Medical College, Albert Einstein and Mt. Sinai.

In defiance of the dean, a Cornell Medical College committee of three department heads (Dr. Walsh McDermott, public health; Dr. Walter Riker, pharmacology; and Dr. Robert Pitts, physiology) and three medical students sponsored a proposal in November 1968 that the school would develop a program in the 1969–1970 academic year to admit "disadvantaged students" comprising not just a token number but approximately 12 percent of the entering class; that the director of that program would be black and a full-time faculty member with experience in the fields of medicine, medical education, and counseling and administration; that the director would be a member of the dean's staff and also have a faculty appointment; that a special program in the summer following their junior year would be developed for minority students; and that full financial aid would be offered to entering minority students in need. The faculty-student group that made the proposal, which was promptly adopted by the faculty council, was also the search committee for the director. In the spring of 1968, I was invited for an interview.

This country has had a long tradition of preferential admissions to colleges and universities. Public colleges and universities offered what almost amounted to open admissions for qualified in-state applicants, who were charged little or no tuition, while out-of-state applicants faced higher admissions hurdles and invariably paid more. Private colleges and universities, first and foremost, favored applicants from alumni families, many of whom were capable of only a "gentleman's C" grade-point average but enjoyed the certain knowledge that they would nonetheless graduate into a leadership position in the national professional old-boy network. Applicants who were talented in athletics but not in the classroom were welcomed despite below-average academic credentials, and often allowed to take easy courses with heavy tutorial support. The prestigious private universities like Harvard, with a mission of educating future leaders of the nation, modified their admissions criteria for students who came from different geographic regions of the country, realizing that bright students educated in areas with fewer educational and cultural resources would not enter with qualifications like those of their more fortunate peers but would, in a more enriched learning environment, soon equal them in achievement. This is the same logic that the most prestigious medical and other professional schools used as a basis for increasing the enrollment of underrepresented minority students whose intellectual potential had not been actualized because of inadequate, racially segregated public schools or racially unequal higher educational systems set up to prepare them for a separate and unequal society. Given the opportunity to experience superior education, their true potential would be realized as they took their place in the future among the nation's leaders.

In the United States, the term "affirmative action" currently refers to policies that take gender, race, ethnicity, or physical condition (age or disability) into account in an attempt to promote equal opportunity and increase ethnic and other forms of diversity in workplaces and schools. Its primary mission, therefore, is to redress perceived disadvantages due to overt, institutionalized, or involuntary discrimination resulting from entrenched social tradition and cultural practices reflecting the hierarchical order of society. Understandably, any movement aimed at a redistribution of power and influence to a broader popular base will run into a brick wall of resistance from defenders of the status quo and their apologists.

The fundamental logical base and political justification for affirmative action is that the institutions that educate, employ, and maintain law and order and domestic tranquility in a democratic society should be more representative of the population they serve, in spite of the fact that at its birth the United States was quite the contrary: a slave-holding nation ruled by an elite group of white men, property owners and members of the Church of England who proclaimed that we were one nation, dedicated to the proposition that all men are created equal, with the right to pursue a life of liberty and justice for all. This is why Gunnar Myrdal, in his 1944 book *An American Dilemma: The Negro Problem and Modern Democracy,* called this our country's fundamental moral dilemma, that as a nation we should be set on a course of living up to the kind of country we wanted to become.

Affirmative action began in the United States in the late 1960s following the assassinations of the two Kennedy brothers, of Martin Luther King Jr., and Malcolm X, the race riots and burning of black urban ghetto communities, and the worldwide revolutionary movement of students determined to end the Vietnam War and extend civil rights to socially excluded minority group men and women. The term "affirmative action" itself was first used in the United States by President Kennedy in a 1961 executive order that required all organizations holding government contracts to employ persons without regard to race, creed, color, or national origin. Four years later, President Johnson issued an executive order holding government employers to the same standard and signed several landmark civil rights acts, emphasizing that black Americans had to be granted more than rhetoric about freedom, but also jobs and admissions to colleges and universities, because their innate intelligence was stunted by weak families, problem neighborhoods, and poor schools. In 1967, it was also President Johnson who added gender to the anti-discrimination list. President Richard Nixon, in his Philadelphia plan of 1969, required federal government contractors to hire members of minority groups at all skill levels according to strict quotas and timetables, in a cynical effort to drive a wedge between unionized labor, with its seniority rules, and minority groups and Jews, who had formed the leadership coalition for civil rights. Jews had achieved leadership in university education and corporate life because of demonstrated current merit rather than any presumed future qualification. This tension persists.

In 1971, the U.S. Supreme Court ruled, in *Griggs v. Duke Power Company,* that tests to screen job applicants had to be job-related and that the burden of proof was on the employer to show that a test was designed to predict who could do the job and not just to eliminate applicants with less competitive high school educations. The 1978 Supreme Court ruling in *Regents of the University o/ California v. Bakke* brought the issue squarely into the realm of medical schools. Four of the justices wrote opinions upholding the constitutionality of the University of California, Davis admissions committee's program establishing a strict quota of blacks to be admitted and stipulating that they were to compete only with other black applicants instead of the general applicant pool, holding that this ensured these applicants of the U.S. Constitution's Fourteenth Amendment protections by giving them equal access to educational opportunity. Those four justices also wrote that this was consistent with the Court's 1954 decision in *Brown v. Board of Education,* which held that racially segregated education was inherently unequal.

Another four Supreme Court justices in the Bakke case maintained that UC-Davis had provided an unfair advantage to black applicants by excluding white applicants who were better qualified and who might have experienced other life experiences of adversity but had overcome them, and that very strict scrutiny should be applied to justify the use of racial identity to remedy past admission exclusion. Justice Lewis Powell avoided the issue of the Fourteenth Amendment's equal rights provisions in his opinion supporting his deciding vote. He found that faculty admission committees have a First Amendment right to admit a class of students with an array of diverse characteristics in the interest of giving them a broader educational experience, and that race could be one of several such characteristics, but not the only basis for a favorable admission decision. That line of thought remains in force today.

In 2003, the Supreme Court heard two cases brought by white plaintiffs against the University of Michigan claiming that they had been excluded while less- qualified blacks were admitted; that Michigan's undergraduate College of Literature, Science and the Arts had an admission protocol that gave too many automatic points to minority applicants; and that this was an unfair race-based advantage, and therefore unconstitutional. On the other hand, the admissions policy at Michigan's Law School was acceptable, as it used ethnicity as only one of several factors favorably influencing membership in the entering class. Justice Sandra Day O'Connor cast the decisive votes in both cases, using the same logic as Justice Powell.

What this meant was that the issue is still in limbo today, and the center of political controversy. State legislatures, voter initiatives, and lower federal courts in California, Washington, Michigan, Texas, Florida, and Nebraska have all sought to ban affirmative action in hiring or in college or university admissions. A relentless conservative campaign to reverse the 1954 *Brown v. Board of Education* led to Supreme Court decisions in 2006 that even though public school districts in Memphis and Seattle had voluntarily decided to racially integrate their schools, it was an unfair use of race. We have come almost full circle to a situation where, in the minds of some, white people now need to be protected from being discriminated against by blacks. Foremost of those protectors, fervent opponents of affirmative action, are black people like Supreme Court Justice Clarence Thomas, who was admitted to Yale Law School under its affirmative action program, and Ward Connerly, a black businessman who profited from affirmative action but now leads the campaign of the American Civil Rights Institute to protect whites from unfair discrimination.

The central misconception confusing the mind of the general public is a misunderstanding of what it means to be qualified for admission to a medical school, or any other higher educational institution for which the number of applicants vastly exceeds the number of places in the entering class. Among data considered by admissions committees are the applicant's undergraduate grade-point average and scores on the Medical College Admission Test (covering areas of both science and non-science competence), an essay by the applicant describing how he or she has decided on a medical career, and an interview by several members of the admission committee, if the applicant is one of the small proportion to reach that stage of success. A qualified applicant is generally one who not only has high grades and test scores, but also shows signs of broad interest and achievement in other cultural affairs, is able to relate and communicate well with others, and shows potential for leadership in research, teaching, patient care, and community affairs. What the admissions committee tries to do is to predict, on the basis of the applicant's academic and other achievements in his or her first 22 years, what his or her achievement will be in the next 50 years, whether the school would be proud to claim him or her as one of their own, how he or she would be valued by classmates and, eventually, by the profession worldwide.

Thus, a score on an admissions test is but one of a complex set of measures, estimates and objective or subjective impressions, leaving much room for bias and error, especially considering that the applicant and his parents and friends and coaches all have their thumbs on the scale trying to make the applicant look good. From my 12 years as a member of the Cornell Medical College admissions committee, I can report that high grades and scores did a good job of predicting success in the first two basic science years, but approximately a fifth to a fourth of students who excelled were only average in the last two years of clinical work, and were surpassed by students performing less well in the first two years. Twenty years after graduation, the class ranking loses still more predictive power. This should not be surprising, given the fact that all students strong enough to graduate from a highly selective university have already shown a basic level of excellence. The ability to relate and communicate at a high level and work well with other members of the treatment team are brought out more clearly in the last two years of clinical work, where students' interpersonal skills enhance their ability to gain sufficient rapport with patients and their families and gather data from which to make a diagnosis and help patients follow treatment recommendations.

Very selective schools usually decide to consider for admission only those whose test scores were in the top 20 percent, regardless of any other indication of potential success. Such a decision is actually a leap of faith based on the notion that such tests are so cleverly devised as to predict success or failure four years in advance.

It so happened that several decades' worth of national medical college admission test scores already revealed that students scoring at the 99th percentile in all science and non-science areas were no more likely to graduate than those scoring at the 88th percentile, and that the test could not predict whether students finishing in the top fifth of the graduating class would or would not be among the top fifth of achievers in their class 20 years after graduation. In fact, looking at the normal bell-shaped curve of scores, it would appear that 80 percent of all medical school applicants were qualified, with a 90 percent chance of graduating and no way of knowing whether they might be considered, 20 years later, to be the leaders in their field. It would therefore be accurate to consider almost every student applying to selective schools, having graduated with high grades from select undergraduate colleges, as qualified. If you have a thousand applicants and only a hundred spaces to fill, who are the ones to select? One could reasonably conclude that admitting a first-year class broadly representative of the total population would be both logically sound and would best serve the public interest by increasing the prospect that all segments of the public would be served equally well.

In real life, the issue becomes still more complex, but understanding these matters will bring clarity. Admissions committees are only one factor in determining which school an applicant will attend. The applicant also chooses which school of the several to which he or she has applied to attend if selected, based on his or her judgment of which is most likely to meet his or her needs and advance his or her career. There is a definite prestige hierarchy of schools, with little doubt within the profession as to which are in the top fifth or the lower fifth. Even after graduating from medical school, students from the top schools will apply for post-graduate training only to those hospitals whose prestige matches that of their medical schools. Hospitals providing postgraduate training are also definitely ranked, even those formally designated as teaching hospitals. Teaching hospitals in the highest prestige category train not only resident physicians in the various specialties but also third- and fourth-year medical students in their clinical years. Teaching hospitals on the lowest rung of prestige have a preponderance of foreign medical school graduates and very few or, usually, no medical student clerks supervised in training mainly by their residents. The overwhelming majority of American hospitals train neither residents nor medical students. (Further details on these aspects of medical education and training procedures can be found in my 2003 book, *Affirmative Action in Medicine: Improving Health Care for Everyone*.) This background information is necessary for a full understanding of my personal involvement in this most significant program, which has changed the face of American medicine in the past generation.

I had learned of the opening on the Dean's staff at Cornell University by happenstance. The wife of a Cornell medical student was doing her social work placement at a family service agency directed by one of my neighbors, a black woman. The social work student at that agency asked her if she knew of a black physician meeting the description of the person Cornell was trying to recruit and I seemed to fill the bill. I was a psychiatrist; Harvard had already recruited black psychiatrist Dr. Alvin Poussaint to be associate dean in charge of their affirmative action program, and Yale had also recruited Dr. James Comer for a similar position. I was already known for developing a program for black high school students in Brooklyn, who might have the ambition to go into medicine, to be mentored by a group of black physicians and dentists who practiced there. This had brought me to the attention of Dr. Franklin McLean, who led the National Medical Fellowships, a program specifically designed to promote academic career development for blacks; I had in 1949 received one of their earliest fellowship awards following my medical school graduation in 1946. He had invited me to become a member of their board of directors in the early 1960s. The Cornell search committee was pleased to learn of my professional background and development, and of my general commitment to racial integration and political action, and I was formally appointed in June 1969. The Cornell faculty had voted for a goal of having underrepresented minority students make up 12 percent of the entering class, that a new associate dean be recruited to head the admissions program, that the new associate dean be appointed a faculty member in his or her field of medicine, and also be a member of the general as well as the administrative faculty council, and a member of the admissions and all other committees affecting student affairs, and would report directly to the dean of the medical school.

Not everything, however, was rosy. I learned from conversations with friends that I could have made higher demands on Cornell before accepting the position. My salary could have been higher; my title was assistant dean rather than associate dean, and I was given an office within the suite of offices for the associate dean for student affairs, but not a private office or secretary or budget of my own. I shared the services of the two secretaries assigned to work for the associate dean of student affairs, who were disgruntled by the additional work I gave them. Since I had no separate budget of my own, the student affairs associate dean had to approve my expenditures. Within a year and a half, I had rectified all of the above limitations. Having demonstrated my competence, I requested my own private office next door to the suite, with my name and title on the door, my own secretary (and, soon, two secretaries), my own budget, and also the generic title of associate dean, not limiting me to any one area. A month after my arrival, Dean Deitrick, who was ambivalent about my coming, had left the school and been succeeded by Dr. Robert Buchanan. My relations with the new dean and his wife were warm and friendly. The associate dean for student affairs, Dr. Larry Hanlon, who had also been lukewarm about my presence, had unfortunately died of cancer a few months later. His replacement, Dr. Thomas Meikle, became a close friend and colleague, but gave me many a headache with his obsessive worry that our admissions committee might be accepting too many high-risk students.

Before I arrived at Cornell, a ten-week summer research fellowship had been planned there for ten black students from Hampton Institute, a black institution soon renamed Hampton University. The program, hastily designed during a weekend Cornell University board meeting by the Cornell Medical School Dean Deitrick and Dr. Jerome Holland, president of Hampton, who had been a star football player as an undergraduate at Cornell, called for a collaboration between Cornell Medical College and one of the country's strongest black colleges. Members of the Cornell faculty had already been recruited as volunteers to have the students work, usually in their laboratory, on a specific problem in the faculty member's area of research. It was customary for all medical schools to offer such summer research opportunities to faculty members' relatives, neighbors, close friends of their family, or to friends or children of alumni eager to enhance their offspring's chances for admission. Two days a week, after we had lunch together, the students spent the afternoon with me, during which they were informed about health problems in New York's black and Hispanic communities, and met physicians who were leaders in delivering service programs to them. We usually traveled on the subway to visit these programs. At other times, I invited prominent black physicians in the city to meet with us and discuss how their medical careers had developed.

On one such occasion, a friend and neighbor of mine, Dr. Cyril Jones, a black surgeon in Brooklyn and a graduate of Harvard University Medical School, met with our group. Dr. Walter Riker, chairman of pharmacology, one of the Cornell faculty members most closely supportive of our entire program and a leader in its inception, was also present that day. Dr. Jones said in the course of his remarks that a black person should not ever trust any white person. This thunderbolt struck me as outrageous, and you could hear a pin drop in the room. I said I thought this was going too far, and pointed to Dr. Riker as a living contradiction to Cyril's slander. Dr. Riker and I later compared notes on our troubled feelings about this racial slur. I happened to know from a previous conversation with Dr. Jones that he had always been bitter because, although he was a good student and admitted to Harvard, the admissions committee at Tufts had turned him down because he had a fluctuating stutter in his speech and performed poorly in his interview. Being accepted by Harvard never soothed his resentment for having been turned down by Tufts, strange as it may seem.

On another occasion, a white medical student at Cornell, known to be an extreme radical, warned our group that even though they might feel comfortable, they should not be fooled, that Cornell was a racist institution, and they were still considered to be niggers by most of the whites there. Fortunately, such well-meaning but foolish advisors were few in number, or at least mercifully silent. Our Hampton students lived in the regular medical student dormitory, and a number of white students had volunteered to be individual mentors to help them learn their way around the school and the neighborhood, and also how to get discount tickets on weekends to some the best entertainment and movies and Broadway shows. They also took their students with them once a week to one of the New York Hospital wards so they could see how third-year medical students examined and worked with patients.

The Hampton students, eight men and two women, were an interesting group. The five strongest were all from countries outside the United States and were attending Hampton on scholarships from their governments or church groups. They were all chemistry majors and had had an extra year of science studies between secondary school and college. The weaker five were four African Americans, including the two women, and one international student who was more interested in an allied medical field than in medicine itself. All five were biology majors. Cornell eventually admitted the stronger five, along with one American black in the weaker group who had high test scores and a B average. It was becoming clear that black colleges in the United States were no longer attracting the stronger African-American students, who were increasingly choosing to attend predominantly white colleges and universities which were opening up to them as a result of those institutions' affirmative action programs. Even black faculty who had done their graduate work at predominantly white colleges were being recruited to teach in predominantly white schools for the first time, and more and more science faculty, as well as students, at black colleges were coming from India or China or other Third World countries where opportunities were scarce.

These considerations led me to conclude that the summer research fellowship program had to be revised drastically, and could no longer be an exclusive Hampton-Cornell collaboration. Applicants would be welcomed from all colleges, but particularly from those undergraduate institutions attended by white students admitted to Cornell Medical College, mainly the prestige schools of the Northeast.

Dr. Holland had by that time been forced out of the presidency of Hampton by radical black students demanding a greater voice in governance there. He had been appointed U.S. ambassador to Sweden, and later was named one of the governors of the New York Stock Exchange. He was not pleased by my decision. One of his white friends, a leader of a major corporation, telephoned me to offer continued and large funding support if I retained the Hampton-Cornell program that President Holland wanted. I turned him down, and I was supported by the Cornell Medical College dean and faculty, who were persuaded of the soundness of my plan.

The program flourished for the next 10 years. It was soon expanded to 25 fellows, was supported by a growing number of faculty sponsors, and was increasingly popular with minority students, whose enrollment increased to 10 percent of the student body within a few years.

Financial support came from the Macy Foundation, and from federal grants for programs to increase minority enrollment in the health professions. Cornell admitted not only minority students who had gone through our summer program, but an even larger number who had not done so, and who on average had both slightly higher grade point averages and medical college admission test scores than the summer program students. As I also reported in my book *Affirmative Action in Medicine,* the summer research students benefited so much from their experience—living in the medical student dormitory with other medical students and already having a support system of faculty and students with whom they had worked—that the overall academic success of summer program students slightly exceeded that of minority students who had higher premedical school grades and test scores but had not been part of the program.

In retrospect, one of the reasons it succeeded was that the Cornell administration worked behind the scenes to build up my credibility as a leader within and beyond the faculty. I was from the first made a member of all of the medical school's governing committees. Dr. William Lhamon, head of the psychiatry department, nominated me for membership in the New York Psychiatric Society, made up of leaders in the field in New York City and New York State.

Members were selected only by existing members, most of whom were on the faculties of the most prestigious private universities, and the membership and minutes were not disclosed to the general public. When I attended my first meeting at the private men's club where they met, two members conspicuously walked out when dinner was announced, rather than accept my presence. They were privately reprimanded and did remain. This was an example of the inner workings of the private control of psychiatry in New York. I was also appointed one of the five members of the New York City Board of Health, which enforces and revises the health code for the city, where I joined another member of the Cornell faculty, Dr. Walsh McDermott, who had helped lead Cornell into its affirmative action program. And I became a member of several statewide committees that advised the governor not only on mental health or minority affairs but on health affairs in general.

The Association of American Medical Colleges (AAMC) is a national group of all medical schools' leadership that, along with the American Medical Association, staffs the Liaison Committee on Licensing which governs education and practice post-graduate medical programs and all specialty boards and standards for state medical licensing. The AAMC took the lead in establishing affirmative action programs in 1968, along with the rest of the medical establishment, and its Group on Student Affairs had a Minority Student Affairs section, well-staffed and funded, which I served as president for several years. I lost a close election one year for president of the Group on Student Affairs. I was also a member of the board of National Medical Fellowships (NMF). Whereas its mission had been to support only those who wished to pursue a career in academic medicine, it was now more important to black students who wanted to have a career as practitioners in all specialities as well as teaching, training, and research. Also:

- It extended financial aid not only to blacks admitted to predominantly white medical schools, but also to students at historically black medical schools like Howard University and Meharry Medical College.
- It broadened its support from only blacks to other underrepresented and previously excluded groups, such as Puerto Ricans from the mainland United States and low-income Mexican-Americans, Native Americans, and Pacific Islanders. This brought NMF poli-

cies in line with the stated mission of the American Association of Medical Colleges and all the major health care institutions, who solidly supported the goal of increasing the proportion of minority medical students and future physicians until it achieved parity with their representation in the total population. My first book, *Blacks, Medical Schools and Society* (1971), details the beginning phase of medical affirmative action; my second, *Affirmative Action in Medicine* (2003), gives a 30-year progress report on the extent to which its goals were achieved.

When my work at Cornell began in the summer of 1968, no American blacks were enrolled in the student body, one black student from an African nation had just graduated, and a black student from Jamaica who was in his second year chose not to identify as black. A flurry of work by white students and faculty and one or two alumni enabled us to find 25 minority applicants for admission, of whom five were accepted. Three of them enrolled elsewhere, but one American black male student and an American black woman ultimately became members of the first-year medical school class. Tables 1 and 2 are reproduced from my second book.

Table 1 shows that there were 12–15 minority students in each first-year class from 1970 through 1977 (the number of first-year class places increased from 91 to 101 in 1972). Cornell's applicant pool had been approximately 2,500 annually before the school joined the American Medical College Admission Service in 1974, through which an applicant's information was sent to all schools on his or her "hope" list. After that, Cornell's total applicant pool then ballooned to 6,000–8,000 a year, and more than 10 times the number of minority applicants. As table 1 also shows, the grade point average and test scores of minority students who were admitted steadily advanced, but data not shown in this table (but also collected in those years) demonstrated a persistent gap of 75 and 100 points on MCAT scores between minority and nonminority admitted students. These gaps demonstrated the obstacle course faced by minority students. The total student body had voted that students' names be omitted on all tests and examinations, with numbers assigned instead, to prevent favoritism or bias in grading. Examinations in all of the two-year basic science courses were graded in a norm-referenced manner, meaning those on the lower end of the curve received a failing grade regard-

TABLE 1. Cornell University Medical College Minority Applicants and
Admissions, 1969–77

Year	Minority Applicants	Minority Admissions	Minority Science GPA	Average Minority Science MCAT
1969	25	2	2.10	500
1970	92	12	2.80	513
1971	151	14	2.95	536
1972	222	12	3.06	556
1973	292	13	2.98	565
1974	677	15	3.01	529
1975	565	15	3.25	585
1976	496	13	3.30	583
1977	552	13	3.21	601

SOURCE: James Curtis, *Affirmative Action in Medicine*, table 1.

less of whether or not they demonstrated adequate mastery of the material,
which would be the case in a criterion-referenced grading system.

As table 2 shows, 62 of the 121 minority students admitted from 1969
through 1978, from six entering classes, had already graduated in that affirmative action decade (remembering that it takes four years to graduate).
There were three dropouts and three transfers, one to Cornell's graduate
school of medical sciences for a career in medical research and two to other
medical schools. The overall retention rate was 97.5 percent, which far exceeded the national minority student retention rate of 87 percent for the
same decade and almost matched Cornell's non-minority student retention
rate of nearly 99 percent. As of September 1978, seven of the 62 minority
graduates had graduated a year late because they had had to repeat a year;
no student graduated more than a year behind the class with which he or
she entered. Remember also that table 2 includes students who had not yet
reached the fourth year by 1978. The MCAT scores were reliable predictors
of medical school success. Several decades of study had shown that students
with science MCAT scores of 525 had an 88 percent chance of graduating
within four years, those with scores around 625 had a 90 percent chance,
and it was still 90 percent for those whose scores were 725. In other words,
beyond a certain critical range, emotional or social problems cause the small

TABLE 2. Cornell University Medical College Minority Enrollment and Retention, 1969–78

Year	Total Entering Class	Total Entering Minority	Minority Graduates	Minority Transfers	Minority Dropouts
1969	91	2	0	1	0
1970	91	12	0	0	1
1971	91	14	0	0	0
1972	101	12	0	0	0
1973	101	13	1	1	0
1974	101	15	10	1	0
1975	101	15	14	0	1
1976	101	13	10	0	1
1977	101	13	13	0	0
1978	101	12	14	0	0
Total	980	121	62	3	3
Percent		12.3		2.5	2.5

SOURCE: James Curtis, *Affirmative Action in Medicine*, table 2.

proportion of failures, but higher scores are of cosmetic value only. Political game playing and misleading propaganda obscure this reality.

Affirmative action could occur only when historical forces made it inevitable. World War II—caused in part by the punitive sanctions imposed on Germany after World War I, which produced the economic disaster that Hitler blamed on wealthy Jews and used to justify racial genocide—put the United States in the role of protector of all the world's people, bringing democracy, freedom, justice, and economic prosperity to everyone. After the war ended, we were pitted against the Soviet Union, which was making a similar bid for world leadership, in a Cold War which carried with it the threat of a nuclear holocaust that would annihilate humanity.

Within the United States, the 1960s was a time of great prosperity for both corporate leadership and labor unions; we elected our first Catholic President; and a burgeoning civil rights movement united people from all social class, ethnic, and religious groups to create a more inclusive America than had ever before existed. A murderous backlash developed against this vision: assassination claimed the lives of both the Catholic President and his brother, when he later sought that same office; of Malcolm X, who wanted to create a separate nation for blacks within the United States; and of Martin Luther King Jr., who didn't want separate nations for blacks and whites but one nation with liberty and justice and equality for all. His assassination in 1968 and the subsequent riots and burning inner city ghettoes led to more vigorous enforcement of federal civil rights legislation whose goals were highly reminiscent of the landmark amendments to the Constitution that were ratified following the Civil War, which freed the slaves (the Thirteenth), and guaranteed them equal protection of the law (the Fourteenth) and the right to vote (the Fifteenth). All three were essentially nullified by the Supreme Court's 1896 decision in *Plessy v. Ferguson* that upheld state laws racially segregating public facilities under the doctrine of "separate but equal."

This decision produced the situation I described when I was admitted to the University of Michigan Medical School in 1943, the only black in an entering class of 175, which also included only eight women. By 1968, when I was recruited to lead the campaign to admit a more representative proportion of blacks and other underrepresented minorities to Cornell Medical College, there were no American black students enrolled at Cornell. Only about 2 percent of all the country's medical students were black, and 85 percent of them were enrolled in one of the two medical schools set up just after the Civil War primarily to provide physicians for the segregated black American community. The situation had been almost completely reversed by 1975: five times as many of the country's medical students (of whom there were now a greater number overall) were black, and 85 percent of them were in previously predominantly white medical schools while fewer than 15 percent were in predominantly black schools.

What happened was that the passage of Medicare and Medicaid in 1965 necessitated the construction of many new hospitals to care for the millions of additional patients who were now insured. The American Medical Association was forced to stop limiting the number of medical students and physicians; new medical schools were founded and old ones expanded to meet the need for physicians who would receive postgraduate training in these new hospitals. And as the middle class grew, so did college and university enrollments. The need for more physicians in the Baby Boom era after World War II had already led to the admission of more Catholics and Jews, as well as graduates of foreign medical schools, into the nation's medical schools and postgraduate training programs. This affirmative action program to admit more Catholics and Jews was not heralded or noted in newspapers or journals because it was never acknowledged that their exclusions had occurred in the first place. It took the affirmative action initiatives of the 1960s to bring blacks and women into those institutions in significant numbers. Thanks to that pressing need for more professionals, this movement found almost unanimous support from every sector of the American medical establishment, including the American Medical Association, the formerly all-black National Medical Association, the Association of American Medical Colleges, and the American Hospital Association. As I described in great detail in my second book, it was a case of a rising tide lifting all boats. More medical students of all kinds were being admitted to these larger and more numerous schools: white men as well as previously excluded white women, as well as underrepresented minority students, as well as overrepresented minority students like Asians.

The effects of affirmative action in terms of minority college enrollment hit a ceiling in the mid- 1970s. Minority enrollment has stalled at roughly 5 to 7 percent for blacks and 5 percent for other underrepresented minority groups since then. This reflects the inferior quality of life and the inferior quality of elementary and high school education these groups receive; thus these groups cannot produce the 15- to 20-percent proportion that would result from equal educational opportunity. Representation for white women rose from 8 percent to 50 percent because they do receive educational opportunity equal to white men. The fact that there are proportionately fewer well-prepared black students means that competition for them is keener among medical schools, which will not (and should not) admit students who are unable to graduate and perform adequately in their postgraduate specialty training. Since medical schools all compete to enroll underrepresented minority students with high test scores and grade point averages, this means they offer a higher proportion of acceptances to those few, which opponents of affirmative action then brand as reverse discrimination, and results in the claim that whites and Asians are being treated unfairly.

The burning question on many tongues at the start of affirmative action admissions in the late 1960s was, "Yes, but will they return to the ghetto once they graduate and are trained?" My second book attempts to answer that query in the only acceptable way, with scientific methodology. It presents a 30-year progress report on the fields of medicine in which these students were practicing and their practice location. I identified a random sample of 2,000 disadvantaged minority students and a similar number of nonminority students who had graduated in the 1970s, and their practice pattern 25 to 30 years later. The minority physicians clearly located their practices in zip codes where others of their group lived, and nonminority group physicians located their practices primarily in middle-class zip codes. In other words, both minority and nonminority medical school graduates have predominantly returned to the ghettoes from which they came. This is not surprising, given that their support systems, families, friends, and neighborhood colleagues also live there. Both groups were almost all specialists, as has been true of physicians in general since the end of World War II. Blacks were held back from specialization for decades because almost all of them had been confined to the two predominantly black medical schools and excluded from postgraduate training teaching hospitals where specialists are trained, essentially until they began to attend predominantly white medical schools. Affirmative action in medicine could not occur until the higher education system began to be desegregated in the late 1960s. Affirmative action in medicine is mirrored by similar advances in the representation of blacks and other disadvantaged minorities in the fields of law, engineering, business administration, and other professions.

Many older members of the black community do not react positively to the fact that black colleges no longer attract the great majority of strong black students, as occurred in their day. Some of these formerly black colleges have become racially integrated in recent decades. The Howard University College of Dentistry has been predominantly white since the 1970s. The National Association of Graduate Colored Nurses merged with its white counterpart, the American Nurses Association, in 1951—although, in the flush of the black power movement, the National Black Nurses Association was organized in 1971. Problems remain in the states of the former Confederacy, which not only established separate colleges and universities for blacks but also paid for their tuition and living costs to attend professional schools in the North when no professional school was provided for them in their own state. The 1954 *Brown v. Board of Education* decision, which prohibited racial segregation in public schools, also threatened the survival of separate higher education. Many black educators at all levels, from elementary through college, were in danger of losing employment because they lacked the credentials of whites who had been better prepared, and legal struggles persist to fund southern black colleges at equal levels and integrate them rather than eliminate them. Likewise, many black students attending formerly all-white colleges and universities during the Civil Rights revolution of the 1960s demanded separate black dormitories and separate black studies departments, sometimes excluding whites. These quandaries and quagmires remain as obstacles to further racial and social class and sexual integration of our nation.

In my second book I also draw special attention to the historical perspective on Affirmative Action in this country and worldwide. Robert Fogel, the co-winner of the 1993 Nobel Prize in economics, believes that inequalities between the sexes and ethnic and social class groups are likely to shrink in the long term because that's already been happening over the past two centuries. Statistics on height, weight, and longevity in Great Britain show that the gap between the richest social class and the poorest has almost disappeared in the last 100 years. Comparable statistics in the United States for the same time span show a similar closing of the disparity between whites and blacks in health, longevity, education, income, home ownership and, of course, representation in the professions and politics, as well as in sports, entertainment, and other areas of American life. As the world increasingly becomes one community, the need to be a more fully diverse nation, with equal opportunity for persons of all racial groups, all sexual orientations, and all social and economic classes will become ever clearer.

Bulletin and Calendar of Events
The New York Hospital-Cornell Medical Center

1300 YORK AVE., NEW YORK, N. Y. 10021

Vol. 11, No. 25
March 9, 1970

SECRETARY OF STATE ROGERS TO ADDRESS CORNELL CONVOCATION;
DRS. CURTIS AND MCDERMOTT ALSO SCHEDULED TO PARTICIPATE

U.S. Secretary of State William P. Rogers, a 1937 graduate of
Cornell University Law School, will address the third annual
Cornell Convocation on Saturday, April 18, at the Rockefeller
Center-New York Hilton Hotel, 54th Street and the Avenue of
the Americas.

The theme of the all-day session is the interrelationship of
science, society, and the environment--and two members of
the Cornell Medical Community will help probe the various
issues involved. Dr. James L. Curtis, Assistant Dean and Associate Professor of Psychiatry, will be on a panel dealing with
"Man and the City," while Dr. Walsh McDermott, Livingston
Farrand Professor and Chairman of the Department of Public
Health, will serve on a panel discussing "Man as a Biological
Being."

Other panels will consider "Technology and the Environment,"
"Man and Space," "Art and the Public," and "Man and his Val-
ues." These panels will constitute the morning's program.
(continued on p.2)

After the luncheon and Mr. Roger's speech, University President Dale R. Corson will moderate a round table discussion
about the role of the humanities in the technological society.

Tickets for the entire program, including cost of the luncheon,
are $8.50 per person. For further information and ticket res-
ervations, contact Mrs. Anne Bloemen, Public Affairs Associate,
825 Third Avenue, N.Y., N.Y. 10022, tel. 838-4131 or the CUMC
Public Information Office, ext. 7211. All members of the Cornell
Medical Community, their families and friends are invited to
attend.

DISTINGUISHED VISITOR

Dr. William B. Castle, Distinguished Physician, Veterans Admin-
istration, and Francis Weld Peabody Faculty Professor of Medi-
cine of Harvard University, has been chosen to be this year's
Visiting Professor in the Department of Medicine's Mary W. Barr
Distinguished Visitors Programme. He will spend a week at the
Medical College next month.

WORLD TRAVEL

Application forms for group charter flights to Europe this summer
are available at the Office of Public Information and Alumni Affairs, C-140. Students, alumni, and staff members are eligible
to participate in most of the programs.

NEWS OF THE STAFF

Dr. Ari Kiev, Clinical Associate Professor of Psychiatry (Social
Psychiatry), delivered a paper on "Crisis Intervention in Industry" at the annual meeting of the New York State Society of In-
dustrial Medicine with The Occupational Psychiatry Group on
December 10 in New York City. He also gave the keynote address, "Suicide Prevention," at the Multidisciplinary Conference
on Identifying Suicide Potential, held on December 12 at Columbia
University Teachers College....Dr. Bernice Grafstein, Associate
Professor of Physiology, participated in a conference on Regen-
eration in the Central Nervous System sponsored by the National
Paraplegia Foundation, in Palm Beach, February 5-6....Dr. Willi-
bald Nagler, Assistant Professor of Medicine, was invited to address the ENT staff of Lenox Hill and Manhattan Eye, Ear and
Throat Hospitals on "Electrodiagnostic Studies in the Prognosis
of Facial Palsy."

FIGURE 4-1. During my
years at Cornell University
Medical College 1968–1980
I was recruited to develop an
Affirmative Action program
to enroll minority students
into medical school. This is an
announcement of a program of
a special convocation program
in which I participated.

FIGURE 4-2. The announcement that I was elected President and Board Chairman of the National Medical Fellowships, which provided financial aid to medical schools with Affirmative Action admissions programs.

NMF fellows from Cornell Medical College are deeply involved in a project at New York's Julia Richman High School in which they identify and counsel students with the trait for sickle-cell anemia.

have the trait, while one out of 500 Blacks actually carries two genes and for this reason has the disease. Because the malady has its onset in infancy, the Cornell students did not expect to find undetected cases of the illness but concentrated instead on determining whether those tested were carrying the sickle-cell trait. If two such carriers marry and have a child, chances are one in four that the child will inherit the disease.

The screening procedure is simple. A drop of blood, obtained by pricking the finger, is added to two cubic centimeters of Sickledex reagent in a test tube. If the solution clouds, the subject is asked to undergo more extensive blood testing to determine if he is a sufferer or a carrier. Of 534 high school students tested last year, 37 were found to be carrying the gene for the disease. Screening procedures have been carried on again this year, on an additional 401 students, and an additional 28 carriers have been identified.

After a student is found to be a carrier, he or she is invited to participate in counseling sessions directed by the Cornell students. Videotapes, recordings, television monitors and other audio-visual aids have been used to encourage maximum participation in the counseling as well as in the original screening procedure. The counseling sessions serve to answer questions, quell fears and dispel much of the misinformation that surrounds sickle-cell disease. Carriers are not told what to do, only presented with the consequences of their alternative choices.

To measure the effectiveness of education and counseling efforts, a five-year follow-up survey will be conducted with those who have been identified as having the trait. The focus of the survey will be to determine how many persons who subsequently marry ask that their spouse be tested for the trait, how their marriage decision is influenced by this information and how many choose to adopt children rather than have their own or plan to remain childless. A yearly screening of students entering the high school will also be carried out.

FIGURE 4-3. Minority students at Cornell receiving NMF financial aid. Also pictured are the students conducting a Sickle Cell Anemia screening and counseling program at the nearby Julia Richman High School, attended by predominantly all black and Hispanic students. At that time, there was no public high school located in Harlem.

CHAPTER 5

Psychiatric Services in Central Harlem, 1982–2000

IN THE 1950S, HARLEM Hospital, one of 21 member hospitals in the municipal system, was the chief provider of medical care for the community's 400,000 residents, almost all of whom were black. Their average income was less than a third of the citywide average, which meant that almost everyone living there was eligible for publicly subsidized services. Psychiatric services had been nonexistent until 1947, after which they were furnished by four part-time psychiatrists, one social worker, one full-time and one half-time psychologist, and one psychiatric nurse.

They could do little more than provide psychiatric and neurologic consultations, and make provisional diagnoses on patients with acute psychiatric disorders, who were then heavily sedated and transferred to Bellevue Hospital, several miles away downtown, from where they were moved to the state-run Manhattan Psychiatric Center—Ward's Island for inpatient mental hospital care.

It was not until 1962 that the situation began to change, when Dr. Elizabeth Davis, a black psychiatrist who was in the class behind me at the Columbia University Psychoanalytic Clinic for Training and Research, became one of the part-time volunteer psychiatrists assisting Dr. Harold Ellis, the black neuropsychiatrist (more neurologist than psychiatrist) and head of the service, in providing the minimal psychiatric care available. Dr. Davis had superb credentials; she was educated at Barnard College and then at the Columbia University College of Physicians and Surgeons, and completed her psychiatric residency at the adjacent New York Psychiatric Institute. She was also from a black family with many members who were blonde and blue-eyed and could have passed for white, and was the daughter of the Black Episcopal priest of one of Harlem's largest churches. What's more, she came at exactly the right time in history.

Several major forces drove the rapid expansion of the American economy after World War II: manufacturers and other corporations profited by satisfying the pent-up consumer demand created by wartime rationing and shortages; easier credit enabled consumers to purchase homes, appliances, radios (and later televisions), and automobiles; the G.I. Bill of Rights created a new, predominantly white and well-educated middle class, and there was unprecedented cooperation between corporate America and unionized labor. The result was a fivefold increase in the nation's gross domestic product between the end of World War II and 1960.

An infusion of federal funds dramatically increased the nation's hospital capacity as new hospitals were built and existing ones expanded, and receiving those funds required nondiscrimination in staffing and patient admissions. The number of postgraduate medical· training positions in teaching hospitals soon vastly exceeded the number of U.S. medical school graduates, whose quantity had been limited by the American Medical Association in order to maintain its near monopoly of medical manpower. Politics loosened the AMA's grip: the number of medical schools and their class sizes both increased, and Catholics and Jews were no longer excluded from training positions but, as mentioned in chapter 4, hospitals turned to foreign medical school graduates to fill those slots, with little attention paid to the quality of medical education they had received or their facility with English or their ability to communicate with patients. It was not until the Civil Rights movement of the 1960s that women and underrepresented minority groups in the United States gained widespread access to the education and training that had been denied them. Before then, the overwhelming majority of women or African-American doctors had graduated from the handful of medical schools set up especially to educate them. But the passage of Medicare and Medicaid, the creation of the Great Society's neighborhood health clinics, and Community Mental Health Board funding all were aimed at producing a more inclusive America, and with a rising tide lifting (approximately) all boats, affirmative action was popular with the general public as well as the American medical establishment (including the American Medical Association and the American Hospital Association), and was led by the Association of American Medical Colleges, which set standards for the nation's medical schools.

The quality of medical care provided by poorly trained physicians from other countries in the New York City hospital system had reached a scandalous low by the early 1960s, but Columbia University's School of Public Health was in the forefront of finding a remedy. The dean of the school, Dr. Ray Trussel, also was director of the New York City Department of Hospitals. He enlisted the aid of Dr. Lawrence Kolb, chair of Columbia's Department of Psychiatry, who accepted the responsibility of building a department of psychiatry at Harlem Hospital subject to the following conditions: that the new psychiatry department have all hiring, promotion, and firing authority; that it be given funds to hire nurses, social workers, psychologists, activity therapists, and support staff; and that only the support staff be paid from the Harlem Hospital budget rather than the Affiliation budget. With these conditions met, Dr. Kolb selected Dr. Elizabeth Davis, already on the Columbia psychiatry staff, to head the new department. A few years later, after the failure of her first marriage, Dr. Davis married Dr. Trussel. He eventually persuaded the Columbia-Presbyterian medical and surgical services as well as the Presbyterian Hospital heads of the same departments to enter into a Harlem Hospital Affiliation, which would be managed by an Affiliation Office to be located at Harlem Hospital and responsible for quality of care at all the sites. A gradually intensifying power struggle ensued between the office of the Harlem Hospital executive director and the Affiliation Office's director and staff.

During her 15 years as director, Dr. Davis built a department of unusual size and strength with an interracial staff, many of whom had worked with her at Presbyterian Hospital; there was no other department of that quality in the United States or the world serving a predominantly black community. As was customary for American psychiatrists at the time, however, they had little involvement with patients suffering from addictions, although heroin addiction plagued the black community and was a leading cause of death; nor were there programs for juvenile delinquents who came in great numbers to courts, corrections, and so-called state training schools, or for school children with mild or moderate mental retardation, learning disabilities or attention deficit disorders. Almost all patients in the city with these disorders, most of whom were treated by agencies whose budgets were supervised by the State Mental Health Commission, were served by programs not led or significantly staffed by psychiatrists. For several months early in the department's history, a community group in Harlem had not only demonstrated against this arrangement but also occupied offices of the Harlem Hospital psychiatry department demanding that it develop programs to treat drug addiction and that the community group be given a budget and hiring authority to staff and run these programs. None of these demands was met, and eventually the demonstrators desisted and regular departmental functions resumed, but many similar demonstrations were common in that era.

By 1977, Dr. Davis and Dr. Trussel had retired and moved to Puerto Rico, although they spent several months a year in New York City. The mid-1970s saw a failure of the financial and banking interests to handle New York City and state bond debt, and the threat that the city would be forced to declare bankruptcy and surrender financial control to the state, which was heavily in debt itself following Nelson Rockefeller's four terms as governor, during which he spent extravagantly to build a huge state university system, the Twin Towers, and the 19-story Harlem State Office Building (now the Adam Clayton Powell Jr. State Office Building), among other notable ventures.

Unlike any of the nation's other great cities, New York voted to share the expenses of the huge new Medicaid program on a 50-50 basis with the state. It had for decades funded a comprehensive municipal higher education system that enabled residents to attend college virtually for free, as well a vast public transportation system. Moreover, it employed union labor to provide essential maintenance, public health, and hospital services that were unmatched in the nation. The city had tried to cope with the increasing costs of these practices by so-called deficit financing, but it was at the mercy of the banks that held the debt and were threatening to downgrade its bond rating. Governor Hugh Carey and Mayor Abraham Beame appealed to President Gerald Ford, but he refused to provide financial aid to the city, inspiring the famous *New York Daily News* headline "Ford to City: Drop Dead." Thanks to what has been described as masterful political leadership by Governor Carey, the federal government did indeed lend the state $2.3 billion, which it used to fund the Municipal Assistance Corporation (MAC). As a state agency, the MAC could float bonds; it also controlled city expenditures, won concessions from labor unions and their pension funds, and enlisted the collaboration of Mayor Beame in reducing benefits and cutting back on hiring new employees. This had serious consequences for the relatively new Health and Hospitals Corporation, which had been formed in 1969. Its second president, a black physician named Dr. John Holloman, was forced to end or severely curtail services in nine of the 19 hospitals in the municipal system. Mayor

Beame had appointed him in 1974 but forced him to resign in 1977 due to his resistance to these reductions. Dr. Holloman and I were friends; he graduated from the University of Michigan Medical School the same year I entered it. Ed Koch, who succeeded Beame as mayor in 1978 and served until 1989, was outspoken in his desire to scrap the entire municipal hospital system, but the private voluntary hospitals kept him from doing so because it shielded them from having to provide health services to patients who had either no health coverage or Medicaid, with its relatively low fee schedules.

Central Harlem's population had dropped from 400,000 in the 1960s to 230,000 in 1970. This shrinkage was largely due to the flight of the black middle class which had severely weakened the neighborhood's political clout.

From the time I left Cornell in 1980 until I started at Harlem Hospital in 1982, I worked half-time on the child psychiatry service at Metropolitan Hospital in East Harlem, a predominantly Puerto Rican neighborhood, and had seen at close hand not only the increasing political power of the Hispanic community but also how a rivalry was being nurtured to drive a wedge between the black and Hispanic minority groups in New York. Comprising an entire new wing of Metropolitan Hospital, this neighborhood's huge, federally funded Community Mental Health Center was one of the most modern and attractive psychiatric facilities of any kind in town. The Metropolitan Hospital and Community Mental Health Center director, a Jewish psychiatrist named Dr. Al Freeman, had confided to me that when he graduated from medical school in the 1940s, the best internship he could obtain in New York was at Harlem Hospital.

Harlem Hospital's director then was Dr. Louis Wright, a black physician who couldn't even get an appointment to its staff in 1927, despite having graduated at the top of his class at Harvard, because whites headed all the clinical services there at the time as well as comprising the entire administrative leadership. Dr. Freeman was proud of having appointed a black woman, Dr. Phyllis Harrison Ross, as the Community Mental Health Center's director of psychiatry. She and I learned to our mutual surprise that we were both graduates of Albion College.

I noted while working at Metropolitan that they had little trouble recruiting interracial staff to work there, especially on the children's service, and that their services were very popular and heavily utilized by community members. It seemed clear that the Puerto Rican political leadership had been successful in obtaining maximum benefits from the city and state for its constituents, and that more Hispanics than African-Americans were being appointed to the city and state offices that oversaw physical and mental health and substance abuse services. Deliberate efforts to divide minority communities were nothing new in New York City, where government funds have historically gone to neighborhoods controlled by ethnic and religious groups. Rivalries along those lines have long been a feature of city life and politics.

It was therefore not surprising that the position of director of psychiatry at Harlem Hospital was vacant from 1977 until 1982. The Columbia University College of Physicians and Surgeons' search committee could not find a candidate who was willing to accept the job, whose professional credentials were acceptable to Columbia, and who could win the approval of the Health and Hospitals leadership, the Mayor's Office, and the hospital's all-black Community Board. Columbia had proposed a white woman psychiatrist on their faculty as director, who would be assisted by two black psychiatric residents who had recently completed their training and were on the staff of one of their community mental health centers, but the Community Board would have none of it. Overtures had been made to me by members of Harlem's medical staff, especially Dr. Margaret Haegerty, the director of pediatrics, a white physician who had known me when we were both at Cornell and New York Hospital, but I was not convinced it would be a good move for me. I had long believed that ideally there should not be a separate hospital system for the poor, black or white, but that all income groups would be better served in the same system. True as that was and is, it was and is also true that in New York City, health and hospital services, even for the poor, are distributed on the basis of neighborhoods that are dominated by the religious and ethnic groups who live in them. What this means and meant was that a given neighborhood will have only as much as its clout can get, and Central Harlem lost a lot of influence when its middle class population nosedived. This overwhelming reality was the main reason I decided, after more than a year of vacillation, to accept the position of Harlem Hospital's Director of Psychiatry.

When I arrived at Harlem, I was pleased to find that the Department of Psychiatry still maintained its own separate affiliation contract with Columbia University, and that essential features of the department remained under the control of its director and administrative staff (as Columbia's director of psychiatry had insisted). Not only did the director of psychiatry recruit, hire, and promote psychiatrists, of which there were 35 (two-thirds of them full-time and board-certified), but he also appointed and supervised the director of the residency program and its 32 residents. The director also selected the heads of support disciplines such as nursing, social work, and activity therapy; and the department's administrator also had final authority in hiring all of the more than 300 support and maintenance staff, although their salaries were under control of the executive director of Harlem Hospital Center, who was appointed by the Health and Hospitals Corporation.

I gradually became aware that I had been a victim of "bait and switch." Within three years of my arrival, the adversarial relationship between the municipally appointed executive director and the affiliation office director ended badly for me. My chief administrator was no longer a member of my affiliation staff but rather a member of the Harlem Hospital executive director's administrative staff. This left me with direct administrative control only over psychiatrists and the selection and supervision of psychiatry residents. The heads of all of the support disciplines such as nursing and social work and psychology were not selected by me but still required to attend my weekly departmental meetings because, as head of the department, I was responsible for quality of all the clinical services.

Many serious problems had developed in the department during its five years without a director, the most serious of which was that the residency program had been placed on provisional status by the national specialty training board, meaning that the program would be terminated if deficiencies in both what they were taught and how they were supervised in their clinical work were not corrected within three years, and we could no longer train future psychiatrists. My clinical training and specialist certifications were to play a major role in the training redesign, as I was able to be a major teacher and supervisor in all the department's services. This provided my first opportunity to see how much support I could expect to receive from the Columbia University Department of Psychiatry, which had overall authority for assuring the quality of our training and clinical services, and it was considerable. They made me a member of the Columbia psychiatry department's leadership staff, and I was expected to make a brief report of Harlem's progress and problems at its monthly meetings. I was appointed to the New York State Office of Mental Health's Professional Advisory Council, which consisted of directors of psychiatry of state, city, and voluntary private hospitals who met monthly with the New York State Mental Health Commissioner to review statewide problems and possible solutions. I received almost no direct guidance or support from the director of psychiatry at Presbyterian Hospital as to how we should redesign our training program. My director of residency training was scheduled to meet each month with the director of Columbia's residency training program, but received no specific guidance on how our program could regain full approval. Through a contact I made during my meetings with the State Office of Mental Health, I became friendly with the director of psychiatry residency training at New York University and Bellevue Hospital, who volunteered to help us develop a new training curriculum so we could receive full accreditation again. This was, indeed, accomplished within the allotted three years, and our program received high marks in subsequent reviews by the national residency training board.

One of my primary missions in coming to Harlem was not only to develop a strong program of residency training and clinical service but also to make it an important center for psychiatric research. Thus, one of my requirements for accepting the appointment was that I be given resources to develop clinical service research programs to study the most effective means of providing psychiatric treatment to an inner-city patient population. I envisioned building on the five-year experience I had had in Brooklyn as psychiatric consultant to a social work team that provided outreach therapy to a group of 29 multiproblem families with what turned out to be little benefit, producing only minimal improvements in their overall family function. Here was an opportunity to see if adding outreach psychiatric treatment to social service visits would promote better patient outcomes and compliance with the psychiatric treatment planned for them after they were discharged from the hospital. I was able to recruit Dr. E. Joel Millman to join my staff as research coordinator when I learned that he was losing his position at Creedmore Hospital, one of the large state hospitals in the borough of Queens. He had received his PhD from Columbia as well as a master's degree from the Columbia School of Public Health. Dr. Millman and I worked closely together throughout my 18 years at Harlem in one of the most productive collaborations of my professional life. Another important supporter was Dr. Elmer Struenig, one of the principal epidemiologists for the New York Psychiatric Institute and a professor in the Columbia School of Public Health, whom I had met while I was at Cornell on one of my research projects there. He invited Dr. Millman and me to meet with him, gave us computer access in his department, and welcomed the prospect of our collaborative research.

Many faculty members in the Columbia University School of Public Health also held appointments in the Department of Psychiatry. Since I received my training at Columbia's Center for Psychoanalytic Training and Research, I had become friends with some members of this Columbia network.

Our clinical services and research programs at Harlem both prospered. Despite continuing budget cuts and reductions in staff, we actually increased the number of our inpatient beds from 37 on my arrival in 1982 to 68 when I left in 2000. This happened largely because the State Office of Mental Health was committed to reducing the number of patients admitted to the Manhattan State Psychiatric Hospital in order to shift responsibility for their care as much as possible to private voluntary hospitals or, as a last resort, municipal hospitals. At Harlem, we usually saw 10 to 20 patients a day in our psychiatric emergency room, half of whom needed to be admitted for inpatient treatment of acute psychotic disorder. Since we ordinarily had enough beds for only three or four of those patients on our inpatient service, the city mandated that we call Metropolitan Hospital, our back-up city hospital, which had almost twice as many beds as we did, to see if they had room. If we were still left with patients requiring admission, we had to contact other hospitals in the municipal system. Manhattan State Hospital also had an acute hospital service, but they had set a quota in the early 1980s of 20 admissions a month from Harlem Hospital's ER. When I left Harlem 18 years later, Manhattan rarely admitted more than two or three a month. In fact, it maintained a large day treatment program, treating several hundred patients daily in an attractive, fully staffed facility located 15 blocks from Harlem Hospital in the huge and handsome Harlem State Office Building. When one of their patients decompensated due to lack of compliance and needed to be admitted to a hospital for acute treatment, their protocol specified that the patient be sent to the Harlem ER rather than to Roosevelt Island, where Manhattan State Hospital is located.

In 1990, Richard Surles, the New York State Mental Health Commissioner and his staff selected Harlem Hospital to partner with Presbyterian Hospital's Psychiatry Emergency Room and become one of the first four psychiatric emergency rooms in the state to be designated as Comprehensive Psychiatric Emergency Rooms. It was to be the first such collaboration in state history between a municipal hospital and a private voluntary one. Each hospital received a grant to renovate its psychiatry emergency room and add six inpatient beds, where patients could remain for up to three days. The grants also paid for additional staff: a general internist, a psychiatrist, and social workers. Increasing numbers of patients were coming to psychiatric emergency rooms suffering not only from acute psychotic illness but also severe substance abuse, usually alcohol in conjunction with several other drugs, especially cocaine. Their ER visits were usually triggered by their substance abuse, and that would be made the focus of their treatment plan. If such patients were unwilling to accept referral for drug treatment, as was often the case, we could only give them counseling and discharge them to the street. Those willing to be referred had to have some form of transitional residential care until they reached to the top of the waiting list for drug treatment. Our designation as a Comprehensive Psychiatric Emergency Room also gave our partnership access to 6 of the 30 beds in the Crisis Residence on the grounds of the Manhattan Psychiatric Hospital, where patients could remain for up to a month while waiting for a residential drug treatment program to accept them. During that time, Manhattan Psychiatric Hospital required that our patients be brought back to Harlem or Presbyterian for day treatment to improve their readiness for drug treatment. Since Presbyterian offered no day treatment for such patients, Harlem was allowed to use all six beds. This new arrangement meant that we were able to provide better care than ever before for patients with both mental illness and substance abuse issues, and our patients' subsequent clinical course was substantially improved. Today, such patients would not have access to this high quality of continued treatment because residential drug treatment currently is reimbursed for no more than 30 days, rather than the six months to two years that is usually required and was covered in the 1980s and 1990s.

My opportunity to do the more significant clinical research I had sought when I accepted the position at Harlem Hospital came toward the end of my first year there. We were awarded a $400,000 research grant by the Robert Wood Johnson Foundation, supplemented by another $200,000 from the New York City Health and Hospitals Corporation, to collaborate with Dr. Struenig and his staff at the New York Psychiatric Institute in researching the effectiveness of outreach case management in reducing the rehospitalization rate of patients who had been discharged after treatment for acute psychosis, with or without concomitant substance abuse disorder. Our study focused on patients with no psychiatric hospitalizations in the previous two years. Dr. Millman and I met weekly with our case management team to review the patients' discharge treatment plans and modify them if necessary. Dr. Struenig and his postdoctoral research assistant met with our Harlem team once a month, while Dr. Millman and I met with Dr. Struenig and his research assistant once a week.

Two to three days prior to being discharged from one of our inpatient wards, patients were randomly assigned to one of three groups: the intervention group, the control group, or the chronically ill group, which Dr. Struenig and his team had already followed for several years. Our case management team reviewed the comprehensive treatment plans for the intervention group and control group patients at the time of their discharge, including medical problems, psychiatric problems, substance abuse problems and social problems. A similar plan was prepared for patients in all three groups, but those in the control group and the chronically ill group received routine treatment and care while Dr. Struenig and his team also continued to provide case management for members of the chronically ill group. Intervention group patients were expected to follow the prescribed ambulatory treatment as well, but one of our main findings was that these patients quickly came to rely persistently on the case management team to meet their treatment needs and refused to go to our regular department outpatient clinic.

We followed these patients for three years, from 1985 to 1988, and published our findings in three papers in peer-reviewed journals. It turned out that more than half of the patients in all three groups had severe substance abuse problems along with their psychotic disorder. The first of these papers showed clearly that despite having no history of previous psychiatric hospitalization, our intervention group experienced relapses and rehospitalization more frequently than expected (during the time of the study, our intervention group had 86 hospitalizations, almost the same as Dr. Struenig's chronically ill group, which had 81 hospitalizations while our control group had only 37 hospitalizations). Our explanation was that both our case management team and the patients' families watched our intervention group patients more diligently, so signs of relapse were detected sooner and were followed up with the only intervention we had available: a hospital bed, rather than a safe, secure and less heavily staffed holding environment. In other words, the reimbursement system was dictating the kind of service we delivered, which was not as good as it would have been in the best of all worlds.

The second paper asked, "Does outreach case management lead to improved physical health and longevity of the Intervention Group by comparison with the Controls?" We were surprised that the answer was negative, but that may have been because patients entered the study continuously over the three-year period, which was too short a time to reveal different mortality rates. However, our physician assistant's scrupulous care in taking care of our patients' physical health needs, often going with them to see their physicians and helping them follow recommended treatment, did not make any significant difference in their health outcomes and those of the Control Group that we measured over those three years.

The third paper sought to answer the question, "Does outreach case management lead to a better quality of life as measured by current instruments clinically available?" Again, surprisingly, the answer was negative. It was easy to observe that, as was the usual practice in American psychiatry at the time, the medication prescribed for our patients was excessive compared to the norm in the early years of our use of these psychotropic drugs and, still today, most of the rest of the world use smaller dosages of these drugs than we use. This high drug dosage left many of our patients appearing to be lethargic rather than sociable, outgoing, and apparently enjoying life. This lowered their overall quality of life score but not enough to be statistically significantly different from the Control Group. In other words, we came close to finding that no treatment at all was better than what was available at that time in psychiatry. Nowadays, articles in professional journals and the general media have raised serious concerns that the entire U.S. population has become overmedicated in the last 40 years. The pharmaceutical industry in recent decades gained permission to market its drugs directly to the public, which would have been inconceivable years ago. Moreover, the extreme reductions in length of inpatient hospital stay, demanded by the insurance industry and the so-called managed care revolution, has forced patients to receive large doses of several medications to qualify for reimbursement for the few allowable days for inpatient care. To be sure, appropriate doses of medication will improve the quality and effectiveness of treatment within four to six weeks, but such lengthy stays are no longer reimbursed. It has become increasingly clear that newer forms of cognitive behavioral psychotherapy, along with relaxation and meditation techniques, are underutilized in the current management of severely mentally ill patients in this country, compared with most other nations, including those in the developing world.

WE MADE SEVERAL SIGNIFICANT improvements in the clinical practice of psychiatry during my last decade at Harlem. Within a relatively short time in 1991, we reduced the proportion of patients coming into our psychiatric emergency room who were restrained, the first in a series of reductions in the use of force and violence in our management of acutely ill psychotic patients. New York City police protocol required that when officers encountered a person behaving in a disorderly and potentially dangerous manner in public, the person should be subdued and handcuffed for everyone's protection (i.e., it is safer for the patient and also prevents the arresting officer from using excessive and brutal force). Once the patient crossed the threshold of our ER, those handcuffs were by protocol removed and it was to be our staff's clinical assessment which determined whether physical restraint was necessary or the situation could be handled better otherwise. In one of our accreditation reviews by the Joint Commission on Accreditation of Hospitals, we were asked what percentage of our patients continued to be restrained by medical order, after police handcuffs were removed, and we found it was about 85%. The reviewer suggested that we consider making it a goal to reduce the percentage to, say, 50% within six months. To our amazement, we found that simply by trying to use less forceful methods we were able to reduce our restraint percentage from 85% to 15% in the first month, simply by clinically quieting and talking down these frightened and angry patients.

Maintaining that low level of physical restraint in our emergency room became a source of pride for us and was, of course, a vast improvement for our patients.

Restraints had been used on our inpatient wards only sparingly since the earliest days of our department; we began providing acute inpatient care in 1962, and our patients were never placed in an isolation room, where they would have been constantly monitored and sometimes also restrained. Only in recent years have accrediting organizations and the American Psychiatric Association leadership banned isolation as a general practice.

At that time, we were averaging about 12 restraint orders a month on our 62 inpatient beds, but we noted that almost half of these were occurring on weekends, at which times nurse staffing levels were lower due to budget restraints. We brought consistent pressure on hospital administration and nursing administration to increase our weekend nursing staff levels but with little improvement.

We also felt that our inpatient length of stay was too long. Our average length of stay of 30 days was less than that of most other municipal hospitals but far more than the range of 12 to 15 days in the private voluntary system. We were therefore at a competitive disadvantage with managed care corporations, which preferred hospitals with shorter lengths of stay. Discussions were under way to bring the municipal hospitals in line with managed care principles in order to survive. One reason for the shorter stays in private voluntary hospitals was obvious: all patients at the leading private hospitals were not only admitted voluntarily but also had to show proof of ability to pay before being admitted; police ambulances brought disturbed and impoverished patients with no coverage to municipal hospital emergency rooms. We knew, however, that we should do our best to set and meet more competitive goals. The facts were that about 70% of all psychiatric hospital admissions nationwide were voluntary rather than involuntary, and the percentage for New York State was 59%. To our embarrassment, our rate of voluntary admissions was close to zero. We increased our voluntary enrollments to 60% within six months. At the same time, we reduced our average length of stay from 30 to 15 days.

How did we do it? When an acutely ill patient was brought to our emergency room, hopefully with a family member or friend, our emergency room staff called them to a conference room when the patient had been quieted as much as possible, and we explained to them that we should make a decision together as to how long it would take for the patient to be discharged. The patient was usually already known to our staff from previous admissions, and our staff and the patient's friends and relatives usually knew why the patient had relapsed; we would send our emergency staff's estimate of how long the hospitalization should take to our inpatient service. It was no wonder both voluntary admissions and cooperation with treatment plans soared. Unfortunately, our readmission rate within 30 days of discharge was about 11%. This was twice as high as other municipal hospitals, but their average length of stay was about twice as high as ours. This caused a great deal of controversy, but I was willing to be unpopular for the sake of what I thought to be better clinical practice. My approach was seen as just another example of my incorrigibility, which led to a mutual parting of the ways by the end of 1999.

This chapter will end with the story of the twin plagues that afflicted the Harlem community in the nearly two decades I was there: the AIDS epidemic and heroin addiction. I'll begin by explaining some basic facts about the Human Immunodeficiency virus (HIV), one of the most serious of all sexually transmitted diseases. Its severity became manifest in this country in the early 1980s, when it was first understood that the HIV virus attacked the body's CD4 lymphocytes, the source of the immune system that protects us from infections as well as killing the new cancer cells which regularly form in all of our bodies. This virus can be transmitted to an uninfected person only by an exchange of bodily fluids—such as semen, vaginal fluids, rectal mucosa exudate, breast milk, or contaminated blood on needles or other injection paraphernalia used by intravenous drug abusers—with an infected individual. A few days after contact, a newly infected person may experience non-specific flu-like symptoms.

Although these symptoms go away spontaneously, the virus begins to multiply rapidly throughout the body. It may take 2 to 15 years before the signs of Acquired Immune Deficiency Syndrome (AIDS) appear. All during that long time, an infected person can unknowingly transmit the disease to sexual partners or persons with whom needles are shared. Even newborn infants can become infected as they pass through an infected mother's birth canal.

Within three months of the initial infection, the body's immune system will have produced enough antibodies to destroy the virus, but this virus mutates rapidly as the body creates new antibodies against it, and this struggle goes on for years. A blood test of the infected person for HIV infection during all of those months will show positive. Men who have sex with men were the first group in which the diagnosis appeared, but since no known treatment existed, this vulnerable but often socially powerful group resisted the stigma and discriminatory treatment that would result if their infected status were to become known, as it could make it impossible for them to purchase health or life insurance, obtain employment, rent an apartment, or avoid personal isolation.

Ordinarily, sexually transmitted diseases, like syphilis and gonorrhea, by law had to be reported to the state health department, and proof of treatment had to be produced prior to obtaining a marriage license. Moreover, all newborn infants were tested and, if found to have been infected during childbirth, had to be treated for sexually transmitted disease to prevent serious subsequent illness. HIV infection was different, because there was no treatment for it and only palliative treatment for AIDS. Those wishing to know if they were HIV-infected could be tested (but, in New York, only in a State Health Department laboratory) and there were two stages in the procedure: an initial test to see if the virus were probably present, taking one to two weeks, and an additional confirmatory test, which would take up to another two weeks. Activist homosexual groups demanded that no one could be tested without seeking it and undergoing two phases of counseling: the first to outline to the patient the pros and cons of finding out whether they were infected and, if so, a second phase explaining how to avoid infecting others and best manage their subsequent medical care needs. This would clearly have a chilling effect on the participation of persons who were well aware of their potential future victimization. Moreover, state health departments were only required to report cases that had been diagnosed as AIDS to the federal Office of Infectious Diseases, not those whose lab tests revealed they were HIVinfected and possible carriers of a then-fatal disease (a serious conflict between privacy and public health). Not until 1988 did the first treatment drug appear, when AZT (also known as zidovudine), was found to reduce the infection rate of babies born to HIV-infected mothers if they received the medication just prior to labor and delivery. Since effective antiviral medications began to be available in the mid-1990s, federal health authorities have required that anyone past the age of puberty seeking treatment in a medical facility be tested for HIV infection (results can now be known definitively within an hour), unless they refuse even after counseling. Treatments are now so effective that HIV infection, though still not curable, can be controlled.

During the past 25 years, when a patient complies with treatment, their life expectancy has risen to be almost as long as that of a person never infected. And it is of great significance from a public health perspective that persons receiving treatment are almost completely unable to infect anyone else. But during the many years that I served at Harlem Hospital, the only effective means of preventing the spread of this disease was through preventive counseling preceded by testing, and the efforts I exerted to implement that were among the most frustrating and also exhilarating of my psychiatric career. In other words I ran against the current and attempted to have patients tested as soon as they were willing to do so, and to counsel them against knowingly infecting others or their newborn infants even before effective treatments became available. This made me unpopular in many quarters.

By the mid-1980s, AIDs had become the leading cause of death in the United States for men 25 to 45 years old, and more than half of AIDS victims were black or Hispanic, as were 90 percent of mothers with children who had AIDS, excluding those who had been infected by contaminated blood transfusions. Almost 10 percent of babies born to infected mothers in New York City were testing HIV positive at birth, and more than half of these infected newborns were in Harlem.

Harlem Hospital admitted about 35 AIDS patients a week, with an unknown additional number of infected patients because routine HIV screening was not a part of standard admissions procedure. There were special problems associated with discharging infants who were infected or showing signs and symptoms of disease, such as mothers abandoning their babies and refusing to bring them home; their numbers were piling up on the pediatric inpatient wards. Clearly, a public health emergency existed, more so in Harlem than in any other community in the State. Intravenous drug abuse was a major reason in Harlem, more so than men having unprotected sex with infected men, which was the leading cause in other communities.

In those years Methadone Maintenance Treatment (MMT) was known to be the most effective treatment for heroin addiction. Although it did not cure the disorder, it was determined to be the most effective corrective measure by federal health authorities and the standard-setting National Academy of Medicine.

When injected into the bloodstream, heroin produces a euphoric high which lasts three to four hours, but tolerance develops quickly and ever higher dosages are subsequently required to match the effect of that first high. By contrast, the person who takes methadone orally in front of the nurse at the medication window will be free of craving for 24 to 36 hours. This makes it possible for the addict to come to the clinic, daily at first, and once an effective maintenance dose is established, the addict will feel comfortable and have free time to pursue a meaningful and productive life, rather than constantly needing money for his habit and committing crimes or stealing from family members or friends to obtain it.

Not surprisingly, MMT was found effective in reducing the rate of HIV infection as well as hepatitis C, since both are spread by sharing needles with an infected addict. The best of these MMT programs, like the ones we offered at Harlem, had primary care physicians, social workers, and psychiatric consultants with regularly scheduled hours to assess the severity and interaction of the addict's physical, psychiatric, social, and legal problems and make a treatment plan suitable for his or her particular combination. The patient and the treatment team then came to an agreement as to which staff member would work with the patient on what problems within a prescribed time period. When the American Board of Psychiatry established the new subspecialty of addiction psychiatry in 1994, the head of our emergency service and

I were the first of the 94 psychiatrists to be certified in it. Two more of our attending psychiatrists joined us the following year.

We also studied the attitudes and behaviors of our MMT patients and the counselors treating them at our four offsite clinics in Harlem, the results of which were published in the *Journal of the American Medical Association* in 1989. The state of New York provided HIV testing only to persons seeking it voluntarily, with the stipulation that neither their name nor other identifying information would be known by the laboratory doing the test. The other way the HIV test could be administered was termed "confidential," rather than anonymous, meaning that the patient had requested the test from a private physician who agreed not to reveal the patient's identity without his or her written consent, or had elected to have it in a medical clinic or hospital as a part of a medical workup or in preparation for surgery, with the understanding that the results would be placed in the patient's confidential medical chart so that all personnel who might come into contact with the patient's bodily fluids would be aware of the need to use infection control measures.

Of the approximately 70 percent of our 1,400 MMT patients who voluntarily responded to our questionnaire, 21 percent said they had received anonymous testing but none had received confidential testing. Moreover, in not a single instance had the patient sought this testing on the advice or suggestion of our treatment staff, nor had the treatment staff been informed of the test result, nor had the staff recommended the test. There had been no previous article that reported what percentage of MMT patients was asking to be tested for HIV infection of any kind, nor of any MMT program staff recommending testing or knowing of test results. In short, it was a potentially lethal case of the blind leading the blind, one of our previously unreported findings. Both staff and patients knew almost all the risk factors, and that the two main ones were sharing needles with an infected addict and having unprotected sex with an infected partner. About 80 percent of our 58 staff members answered the questionnaire. Only 15 percent believed that patients were on their own in reducing risk-taking behaviors, whereas 49 percent of the patients believed the opposite. It was truly surprising that neither situation had been previously reported, considering that, especially early in their treatment, patients were required to see counselors as often as five times a week, depending on their compliance with clinic requirements.

There were no easy generalizations to be made about the patients in the study. In terms of education, they were almost equally divided among those who had dropped out of high school, those who had graduated high school, and those who had had at least a year of college. We knew from our own files that approximately 20 percent of all our MMT patients had had some college education, but in our study sample it was 32.4 percent; in other words, a significantly higher percentage of the educated patients answered our questionnaire. Overall, about 90 percent of patients reported that they had shared no needles with anyone in the current year, compared to 81 percent in the preceding year. As for sexual activity, about 29 percent said they were celibate in the current year, and 62 percent were monogamous, which were smaller percentages than the previous year in both cases. A total of 68 patients had been celibate the year before, compared to 145 in the current year, and there was an overall general decline in numbers of sexual partners.

We learned more by seeing what happened when needle sharing and a high level of sexual activity coincided. Generally, the rate of needle sharing went hand in hand with the number of sex partners, reaching such levels that roughly half a dozen patients shared needles with 13 to 35 others and also had 16 to 50 sex partners in a given month. Such patients knew the risk they were running of becoming infected, but the fear it instilled in them was not enough to improve their behavior, which is usually the hallmark of clinically dangerous self-destructiveness requiring involuntary hospitalization or isolation to protect themselves and others.

Clinical studies and our own observations at the time showed that one-fifth to one-quarter of addicts also suffered from clinically severe psychiatric problems, especially depression, with histories of suicide threats or attempts requiring brief hospitalization and subsequent treatment, to which they seldom adhered. These problems were usually secondary to their use of one or, more often, several substances, along with heavy drinking and chaotic personal relationships.

In May 1987, New York City Health Commissioner Stephen Joseph asked me and a small group of other black physicians to his office to discuss the twin crisis of AIDS and heroin addiction in the black community, ending with an invitation to submit our suggestions for an appropriate response to him. We knew that he was planning to initiate a needle exchange program in the city, under which heroin addicts could go to health department offices and pick up clean needles in return for their used ones. They would not be tested for HIV infection or counseled about it, but they would remain in the needles program until they could enter drug treatment, preferably MMT. The presumption was that patients had to wait weeks or months before entering MMT because there was such a long waiting list.

The program was, in my opinion, a publicity stunt to divert attention from considering a truly effective program, which would test for HIV infection and counsel both the addict and his or her close contacts, who also needed to be tested. My private conclusion was that a deliberate effort was being made to conceal the actual number of people infected with the HIV virus, although the Centers for Disease Control had said from the earliest years of the epidemic that any geographic service area or medical facility with as much as a 1 percent incidence of AIDS (the end stage of the disease) in its population should include HIV screening, testing, counseling, and appropriate treatment referral as part of its routine medical workup. There was every indication that the entire Harlem Hospital patient population exceeded that threshold, but the leadership of the Health and Hospitals Corporation refused to act on it, and I surmised the reason was that there was not enough money to pay for the serotesting and counseling which could absolutely prevent this fatal disease, even in the absence of effective medication. While I did everything within my power to make this message known, I encountered increasing resistance, which evolved into attempts to shut me up. So I appealed to the black political leadership in Congress, gaining the support of Representatives Charles Rangel and Floyd Flake, as well as Manhattan Borough President David Dinkins, Special Narcotics Prosecutor Sterling Johnson, the influential black newspaper *The Amsterdam News,* and the black clergy leadership, which had presented signed petitions to Mayor Koch and State Health Commissioner David Axelrod. The needle exchange program was launched nonetheless and it failed miserably, with only a handful of addicts signing up. The idea that a gimmick like this would be the salvation of the black community was both insulting and a disgrace, but well-intentioned people hailed it as compassion.

In reality, there was no waiting list for addicts seeking methadone treatment; Harlem admitted all acceptable patients within two days of their application. Drug dealers in Harlem usually included clean needles with the powdered heroin they sold in a glassine envelope, and other addicts sold clean needles they had stolen from drug stores or obtained from diabetes patients who used them to inject insulin. When David Dinkins became mayor in January 1990, one of his first acts was to terminate the needle exchange program, but these programs continued to operate underground in New York City despite the local ban. The same was true elsewhere as well; the ban against federal funding for them was lifted in 2009. And preposterous claims for the success of these programs are still made, although research had shown that addicts had been changing behavior on their own since the 1990s without any staff intervention of any kind.

My research staff and I wrote a proposal for a voluntary screening and testing program, not only for patients entering our MMT program but for anyone admitted to any clinic or emergency room or inpatient ward on any service at Harlem Hospital. The Johns Hopkins University Hospital, located in black, inner-city Baltimore, had already found that as many as 10 percent of the patients in its general emergency room, almost all of them black, were HIV infected.

Our proposal was that, at a cost of $1.25 million a year, we could test, screen, and counsel all incoming new patients at our medical center. Department of Psychiatry staff would interview and assess the patients and formulate treatment plans for effective preventive counseling. This proposal was submitted to all the appropriate city agencies, and strong letters of support came from the dean of the Columbia University College of Physicians and Surgeons, their director of the Department of Psychiatry, and the dean of the School of Public Health at Columbia. Harlem Hospital's Ethics Committee voted for it, and it was forwarded to the Research Committee of the Health and Hospitals Corporation, whose approval was necessary before it could be submitted to the National Institutes of Health. When that committee (to me deliberately) delayed approval until the last day proposals could be sent, ours was disqualified for being a day late.

We received a sort of consolation prize in 1990, a two-year service grant from the city Department of Health that made it possible to reduce the caseload of the counselors at one of our four MMT clinics from 50 patients to 35. This allowed them to counsel not only patients but also family members who were willing to participate. We also were able to hire a primary care physician. The percentage of new patient enrollees who were HIV positive had already begun to decline, and fell from 44 per cent in 1990 to 23 percent in 1997; addicts were changing their own behavior, as our previous research had shown. A major factor was that addicts were giving up intravenous injection of heroin in favor of smoking crack cocaine, which had become by far the drug of first choice, especially among younger users. Perhaps the most dramatic finding was that when our Department of Obstetrics and Gynecology offered AZT treatment to women in its clinic for prenatal care in 1994, only 10 of 50 accepted.

Of those 10, only one gave birth to an infected baby, while nine of the 40 who refused AZT treatment delivered a child testing positive for HIV. Contrast this with what we found for women enrolled at all four of our MMT clinics during the 1990s. Federal regulations required that all women attending a methadone clinic be tested for pregnancy every six months. From 1988 to 1993, we averaged six to eight pregnancies annually among the 150 women of child-bearing age in the one clinic of ours that we could follow more intensively. (We were only able to focus intensively on one clinic because the grant did not allow the reductions in caseload which would have allowed fewer patients per counselors and would have also allowed counseling of family members and patients in group sessions.)

After we counseled all the women who might become pregnant on the need for HIV testing, every one of them agreed to be tested, and not a single baby was born with an HIV infection.

Fortunately, federal regulations since 2006 have required that all pregnant women be tested without any special consent beyond what's routine for all patients before receiving medical care, unless they opt out for reasons documented in the medical record. The same is true for all persons above age 13. While health departments expect special vigilance to ensure compliance in health service areas with a high incidence of HIV infection (which are now reported by 35 states), the only health areas exempted are those where repeat testing shows that fewer than 1 in 1,000 patients are HIV positive.

Required case finding presents problems, however, because the states vary in their requirements regarding health insurance coverage for HIV treatment. There is no effective nationwide coverage even under the Affordable Care Act, which still leaves more than 10 percent of citizens uninsured, although that 10 percent is the lowest level ever achieved. Obviously, this burden rests most heavily on unemployed or low-income individuals, particularly those in disadvantaged minority groups.

At the end of 2006, 46 percent of the 1.1 million people living with HIV infection in the United States were African Americans, who represent only 12 percent of the overall population. Rates of new infection for African-Americans have steadily increased since federal monitoring began, even as they have fallen for all other ethnic groups. There is no prospect that these disparities will be erased without special affirmative action efforts aimed at the still segregated black community. Even reducing poverty, increasing the minimum wage, and fixing our broken education system will not be enough to reshape opportunities in the most highly segregated and isolated black communities. My years at Harlem Hospital provide compelling evidence that despite this bleak portrait, special efforts can make a significant difference, but black leadership alone does not have the power to bring about change without the commitment and support of others.

WHAT I VALUE OF what I learned is that one must have clearly stated objectives and plans in order to achieve a worthwhile goal, and periodically document how your whole treatment team can identify what works and what doesn't, and be willing to adjust the pathway to meet your goal. Such an evidence-based group effort will not necessarily be accepted by outsiders with different agendas, so you should attempt to mediate your differences to replace conflict, as much as possible, with at least a shared vision of an outcome that would be in the best interest of all.

Let me give some concrete examples. When Mayor Rudolph Giuliani assumed office in January 1994, one of former Mayor David Dinkins's staff members arranged a reception for me in February, Black History Month, at which I would be honored for my contributions to improving health care in Harlem. Mayor Giuliani knew that I had been a strong supporter of Mayor Dinkins and that he had provided our hospital with sufficient financial support to keep our programs not only alive but thriving. In his speech, Mayor Giuliani talked about what he would be doing to improve life for Harlem's citizens but not once did he mention my name. Just a few weeks later, Mayor Giuliani announced his intention to terminate all MMT programs in the municipal hospital system, of which mine was largest, despite expert medical opinion that MMT was and still is the most effective treatment for heroin addiction. This alarming news came to me at the worst possible time.

One of my concerns had been that a large number of prisoners at Rikers Island, the city's largest jail, were known to be addicted to heroin, among other substances and probably were also infected with HIV, but they received no HIV testing or counseling either during their stay or when they were released back into their home community, which for a huge percentage of them was Central Harlem. It seemed to me that Harlem Hospital, with its large addiction treatment program and my growing interest in preventive counseling for persons at risk for HIV infection, should expect and accept a leadership role. I realized that as an essential first step, these discharged prisoners should have immediate access to a safe, attractive, and treatment-oriented place to live,

where they could be given a treatment plan that met their general medical
health care needs, appropriate mental health and substance abuse therapy,
and help with plans to develop their readiness for employment, and that they
should remain in the residence until they were ready for independent living.

Just such a residence was, in fact, already in operation in Brooklyn, where
a gentleman named George McDonald, his wife, and other associates provided a home for homeless men, many of them addicted to various substances
and with histories of incarceration, under the aegis of the Doe Foundation,
their nonprofit corporation. These addicted men were invited to live in their
residence located in the Brooklyn Armory at no cost for room and board,
with the understanding that it was totally drug- and violence-free and that
they must commit to participating in structured group sessions, run by the
men themselves in various stages of recovery, and in job training for cleaning
and maintenance work. The foundation had contracts to provide janitorial
services (and, later, building renovations) at city-owned facilities, employing
residents who could then earn money to help support themselves after their
discharge. With surprisingly little traditional professional staff, this work program, named "Ready, Willing, and Able," was highly successful in turning lives
around. It enabled many of these men to form or reunite with their families.

The program soon expanded to have residences in Manhattan and Queens,
and Mr. McDonald agreed with me that one was also needed in Central Harlem. I served on his board of directors for several years, but the Health and
Hospitals Corporation never provided funds for us to rent and renovate a
suitable building. As a result of this process, I renewed my friendship with
Dr. Mitchell Rosenthal, who for many years had directed the Phoenix House
drug-free residential treatment programs for adults and teenagers, many of
whom were former addicts or prisoners. Phoenix House did not use MMT,
but its treatment programs eventually led to sustained remission for as many
as a quarter of its clients (which, we both realized, was roughly the same long-
term success rate we found in MMT patients). It seemed that a number of us
were finding that a safe, therapeutic, and caring place to live and develop new
relationships was what worked.

In late 1998, I had lunch at the White House with Gen. Barry McCaffrey,
appointed by President Bill Clinton as director of the Office of National
Drug Control Policy (or "drug czar"). He knew of my interest in developing a program for prisoners returning to Central Harlem from Rikers Island,

and had invited me because he felt my experience with MMT and our plans for transitional and therapeutic housing, work experience, and peer group support and leadership showed great potential for success. The General gave me great encouragement and expressed a willingness to come to New York and discuss the matter with me and appropriate authorities. But when Mayor Giuliani learned of my meeting with General McCaffrey, he instructed the municipal hospital leadership and the executive directors of both Harlem Hospital and the Affiliation Office of Columbia University to advise me to discontinue this project. I was further advised that I needed prior approval from their offices to meet or have written contact with anybody outside the hospital. It was clear to me that staying at Harlem was unthinkable under such circumstances.

For that reason it was a surprise when I was notified that, far from being terminated, our MMT program would receive a $1.1 million grant for enhancements from the Health and Hospitals Corporation, but hopes for a therapeutic residence and collaborative planning program for the prisoners at Rikers Island had to become a "dream deferred." This unexpected grant must have been arranged by silent supporters unknown to me, who did not agree with the way I had been treated. If I had learned one thing with certainty by this time, it was that most important matters are managed behind the scenes by hidden players, who are opposed to transparency in the allocation of public resources for the good of the entire public. The last thing the powers that be will tolerate is that planning be open and visible and with the participation of the leadership and citizenry of the area involved.

WITH THE PASSAGE OF years I can see more clearly how some of my views were changed dramatically for the better because of those 18 eventful years at Harlem Hospital. When I came in 1982, the psychiatry residency training program was only provisionally approved by the national accrediting agency, and it was my belief that the major flaw was that the overwhelming majority of the residents were graduates of foreign medical schools, many of which had standards which were far beneath those of schools in the United States. Furthermore, almost all of them had come from families of the privileged elite in those countries who looked down on persons of lower status, an attitude I feared would be brought with them when they came here. An even greater handicap was my view that their frequent lack of facility in speaking

and understanding English, and their lack of cultural competence in understanding Americans, and especially black people, would fatally impair their
ability to form effective communicating and collaborating relationships with
black patients.

My reservations and prejudice toward foreign medical school graduates
were totally wrong, reflecting an unfair bias of which I was unaware. Under
the supervision of our attending psychiatrists, including me, these young as-
piring psychiatrists did indeed form close and effective working relationships
with their black patients in spite of substantial cultural and language differences. These psychiatric trainees came from countries like India, Pakistan,
Korea, the Philippines, Haiti, Nigeria, and Ghana. Moreover, 30 or more
years later, many of them have become faculty members at medical training
centers across the United States, and almost a dozen remain at Harlem Hospital's Psychiatry Department; one who came from Pakistan has for the past
few years been Director of the department.

In all my years at Harlem, we failed to recruit for our residency training
even one first-rate American black graduate from a black American medical school. We also never recruited an American black from a US integrated
medical school. By contrast, I had been able to recruit as members of my
psychiatry attending staff half a dozen highly qualified American black
graduates from leading integrated medical schools, including three from my
former Cornell program and three others who I had supervised when they
were pursuing subspecialist community psychiatry training from Columbia
University.

Also, two Jewish leaders in the Department—the Director for Quality
Assurance and Coordination for Research, Dr. E. Joel Millman, and Stuart
Aaronson, an Administrative Director—have helped to hold the department
to its high level of performance since they came to work with me more than
35 years ago. This has been a remarkable demonstration that people coming
from disparate origins can work as effective team members because of their
common humanity. Our department was never short of well-trained white
psychiatrists applying to become members of our staff. The Columbia University Medical Center Affirmative Action Office required regular reports
guaranteeing that we were not discriminating against them because they were
not black. Harlem Hospital gave me the opportunity to experience the full
meaning of affirmative action from the inside out.

FIGURE 5-1. Me receiving an award for services delivered by the Department of Psychiatry in the Harlem Hospital by members of the Community Mental Health Board and its Commissioner, Sara Kellerman, as well as Dr. Louis Marcos, Director of Psychiatry of the NYC Health and Hospital Corporation.

FIGURE 5-2. Me with two of my Harlem Hospital chiefs of service
who had trained in our residency training program years earlier. Dr. Charles
from Haiti (second to left) and Dr. Naidu from India (far left) and four
of our residents then in training.

CHAPTER 6

My Retirement Years, 2000–2017

I HAD TO RETIRE IN 2000 as the Harlem Hospital Medical Center's director of psychiatry because I refused to stop attempting to bring about a more genuine community partnership in its governance. As mentioned in the previous chapter, I realized that there had been a longstanding competition among the city's various ethnic and religious neighborhoods for their fair share, or more, of the federal, state, and municipal tax funds available to support social service, hospital, and educational services for their communities. The large and influential Catholic and Jewish agencies were already strongly supported by both private and public institutions that they controlled, the black Protestant community had no visible organizational presence, and the white Protestant community had a wealthy religious leadership but wasn't specifically concerned with the needs of black citizens. The closest that Protestant leadership came to meeting those needs was the Salvation Army, which had indeed established family and child welfare service programs specifically tailored to, and located in, black neighborhoods, but lacked health or hospital services.

When I came to Harlem Hospital, I was aware that the municipal hospital system, as well as its neighborhood clinics, primarily served the unwritten mission of providing segregated services for a group of citizens who were not really welcome in the private, voluntary institutions, thus shielding them from having to serve patients with multiple needs and low or no reimbursement. As health services became increasingly expensive, the private, voluntary sector was driven to seek as much federal Medicare and Medicaid funding as possible, while at the same time avoiding serving impoverished patients.

The chances for Harlem Hospital's long-term survival seemed to me to be limited, but there was a definite need for a hospital located in Central Harlem, not only for easy access but also because it would be a leading job provider in the community. The only other hospital in the area that might fill the bill was the former Hospital for Joint Disease, a private voluntary hospital loosely associated with Mt. Sinai Hospital but now known as North General Hospital, which was competently led by a widely respected black hospital administrator, Eugene McCabe, and an influential Jewish lawyer, Randolph Guggenheimer. Several black physicians, especially Dr. Harold Freeman, had succeeded in becoming chief of surgery simultaneously at Harlem and North General hospitals, and he agreed with me that a merger of the two hospitals would best assure the survival of both. It was necessary that it remain unclear which hospital had taken over the other, and the merger would be impractical unless the Health and Hospitals Corporation continued to finance Harlem Hospital's services. It would also require that Columbia University be willing to maintain its affiliation and agree to have the new Harlem Hospital become part of its several hospital system. Neither the Health and Hospitals leadership nor the Columbia Presbyterian Hospital leadership approved of these arrangements, and the medical staff at Harlem Hospital thought it best not to pursue the matter. Unfortunately, the black administrator of North General Hospital died suddenly after a brief illness and Dr. Freeman replaced him as its full-time director, thereby losing his connection to Harlem Hospital. My leadership of the psychiatry department at Harlem encountered increasing and unsupportable losses of staff and programs, leading to my conclusion that it was best to retire.

At the same time, my wife's Alzheimer's disease had progressed to the point that she required full-time care. Her placement in a well-run nursing home on Long Island soon became necessary, lightening a great mental and emotional burden for me. I had had to take on all responsibility of running the household, including shopping, cooking, and paying the bills, as she could no longer manage a checkbook or drive. Again I called on my cousin Eula, a practical nurse who was still living in Chicago but was now divorced and also retired from the hospital where she worked for many years. She came to live with and work for us again and it was a Godsend, because Vivian soon required 24-hour assistance in meeting her personal hygiene needs and was becoming unstable on her feet and unable to manage the stairs in our large home.

This was what had forced me to decide that she would require nursing home placement, as 24-hour home nursing care fell far short of what she needed. My last year working at Harlem was 2000, and with such a heavy personal burden, it was filled with sleepless nights and left me depressed and in despair. Her dementia became so gruesome that she had come to believe that I was her father, whom she had adored as a child, and on one occasion she asked if we shouldn't call Jim (that's to say, me) in New York. I concluded it was best to sell our lovely home in the St. Albans area of Queens and place Vivian in a nursing home in Albion, Mich., where I grew up and still had family members. My plan was to purchase a home in Albion, where we would have the emotional support of family members with whom we had remained close. We had spent several weeks every summer visiting family there, as well as one or two months in northern Michigan at a cottage built by my brother Tom near Idlewild (where many middle-income black families from across the nation had summer homes during the Jim Crow era, when they were largely excluded from other vacation areas).

As I settled into my new home in Albion in 2003, I was overcome with sadness at seeing a town in deep despair. The decline of the domestic automobile industry had left this whole corridor of Michigan a wasteland. Once prosperous Detroit was now dangerously violent, with an almost all-black inner city surrounded by wealthy suburbs to which both middle-class whites and blacks had fled. The black communities of Ypsilanti, Jackson, Lansing, Battle Creek, Saginaw, Muskegon, and Benton Harbor were all in ruins.

I learned of one ray of hope in Albion from discussions with my sister Gertrude and my cousin, Pastor Stephen Williams. A remarkable woman named Vera Simpson had moved to Albion in the 1940s after I left. Following her retirement as a secretary at one of the public elementary schools and the death of her husband, she and a small group of her neighbors and friends decided to pool their funds and acquire and remodel a vacant building that had been a car wash and turn it into a social service agency for children and adults: The Vision of Life Social Service Agency. They had won the admiration and support of the entire Albion community, black and white, who began to provide financial support to turn it into an attractive structure. With the help of volunteers from the community and from Albion College, the agency offered after-school tutoring for children, and classes for young adults in shopping, cooking, gardening, sewing, and quilting. I joined their board of directors and provided major financial support, helping them to purchase kitchen and laundry appliances and computers and telephone connections for tutoring and on-line instruction in job skills and employment. I also provided funds for utilities, insurance, and fire and burglar alarms, and (as I explain below) attempted to have them apply for grants to support the failing school system.

My past life experience had solidified my belief in the crucial importance of improving educational opportunity for children from families with low or no income. This should begin as soon as the child was toilet trained, so that by the time the child entered school at age 5 he or she would already have learned to talk and think and act like children from more economically and educationally privileged families. Upon reaching fourth grade, they should be able not only to read with comprehension and pleasure, but also to handle numbers with competence. Ergo, I proposed that our grant funds would al-low the agency to hire a staff which would help parents place their infants in early childhood (and infant) day care (such a program did exist in Albion but was struggling financially due to a shortage of parents able to pay). The grant money would also be used to hire community members as classroom assis-tants in the elementary school to assist the teachers and to maintain relation-ships and communications with the children's parents. Albion had had such teacher aides when federal funding was available in the 1960s, but this vital program was lost when it dried up. I also thought it was necessary to have a school-based health clinic for early identification and treatment of physical and mental problems that could be interfering with a child's ability to learn.

Albion College agreed to support our grant requests, and volunteered to have its staff assist in writing them. I contacted a close friend who had recently retired as one of the officers of the Kellogg Foundation, who also agreed to help us find support. None of these grant proposals ever materialized, how-ever, primarily because the local school board, the superintendent of schools, and several retired black school teachers failed to work with our planning committee to write them. Furthermore, the devastating economic recession that began in 2008 and a lack of state funding support for the failing school system seemed to extinguish all hope for the agency's survival as an expanded community service program.

The Vision of Life agency does, however, continue to function, but with-out the broader mission and program that funds from the grant would have supported if the proposal had been completed. This caused me to become involved in another local social service program, which was led by my niece, Alma, and her husband, Jerome, both of whom had worked in programs serving delinquent youth. Alma had been a direct care worker for five years in the Florence Crittenden Mother-Baby Program for homeless pregnant teens, which had closed for financial reasons several years before I returned to Albion. She and Jerome, along with five other members of the community, had formed a non-profit corporation, later named Alma's Home for Girls, but had been unable to raise money to purchase a residence that could become a group home for these young mothers and their babies. I joined their board and later supplied the startup funds to buy two large residential homes, which had to be completely renovated to meet Michigan state codes for a building that is used in such a way. My attorney made arrangements for me to form a limited liability corporation, of which I am the sole member, which owns these two buildings.

After three years of work, they were ready for inspection and licensure in 2016 and had been dubbed Alma's Home for Girls I and II. Five young mothers will be housed in one building and seven in the other. Mothers may enter either when they are pregnant or after giving birth, and we plan to provide them with transitional housing, a complete set of educational and social services, mental health and substance abuse treatment, if needed. Two professional master's level social workers will supervise four case managers and five direct care workers. The social workers will be responsible for completing the intake and admission procedures, as well as plans for continuing education, job training, parental skills training, and infant day care for up to two years. After the program has operated for two years, I plan to donate the properties to the nonprofit board, which will own and manage it thereafter. It will cost close to a million dollars annually to run the two residences. Fortunately, our program manager will be Mrs. Kim Brown, who served for several years as program manager at the former Florence Crittenden Home in nearby Jackson. We will provide our own custodial staff, and transportation to necessary services for the mothers and infants. For these teenage girls to become pregnant and homeless means they have been trapped in a pattern of self-defeating behavior that has destroyed whatever support systems they may once have had. Since the Michigan Department of Health and Human Services does not have a budget for the kind of program we envision, most of the funding will have to come from probate courts, community mental health agencies, and families with insurance or private means who could pay for their children's stays. We applied for a grant from the U.S. Department of Housing and Urban Development and expanded the age limit for our clients from 14 to 25, because young women over 18 are totally responsible for the safety and care of their infants and themselves, and this older age group represents a significant and special challenge.

Fortunately, we have some influential institutions on our side. We have received crucial guidance and advice from the start from Starr Commonwealth, an Albion-based agency which for more than 100 years has provided a therapeutic residential treatment program for delinquent or troubled adolescent boys and, in recent years, girls. Strong support has also come from the Albion College President Mauri Ditzler, who is committed to building a stronger Albion community, as well as members of his administration and current or former faculty. Other local leaders also recognize this project's potential to bring jobs (for example, we will need to recruit and supervise foster homes that will be needed for mothers and infants who leave our program but are unable to manage alone) and a new spirit of hope to the community. Another key supporter has been the University of Michigan School of Social Work, where Dean Laura Lein and Assistant Professor Sue Ann Savas have provided tremendous consultation support all along. My plan is to continue as a member of the board, and for a short time as treasurer, and help to develop an endowment fund for its future financial stability.

Two years after my return to Albion, I came to the realization that I had not been back in town long enough to be able to become an effective community leader. I felt especially hopeless about the school situation. Albion High School continued to provide a good education for the small fraction of children who were from well-to-do and well educated families, but a pathetic education for the much greater number of low-income black and white students who attended classes only occasionally. Overall, its students had failed to make the yearly progress mandated by the No Child Left Behind Act for eight years in a row. Black and white parents alike were increasingly enrolling their high-performing children in nearby school districts, taking their state per-pupil funding along with them. Albion High was eventually forced to merge with the high school in Marshall, 12 miles away, a largely middle-class white community that welcomed the students not only because they needed the state allocations they brought with them but also because the administration and faculty put in the effort to make it work. Why did they work hard? Because the white students at Marshall High School and the black and white low-income students from Albion had worked well with each other from the start to make it a great success. They set the bar high for the adults in Marshall and Albion, both of which had school superintendents of great ability and imaginative leadership.

Returning to Albion also brought me closer to Ann Arbor, the home of both the University of Michigan and, of course, Albion College, both of which had played such a crucial role in my early professional development. In 1990, Vivian and I had decided that to show my appreciation to Albion College, we would establish an endowed scholarship fund of $50,000 to support minority students, preferably from Albion, who showed promise of making a significant contribution to any field of graduate or professional study. In addition, the 10 percent annual interest income would be payable not to us but to the fund, the entire proceeds of which would go to the college after our deaths. I have added an additional $5,000 per year since 2005 to the endowment's principal.

It was disappointing to learn in 2012 from the chief development officer at Albion College that they were having difficulty finding a suitable minority candidate from the Albion community, and we agreed to enlarge the area of eligibility to include all of Calhoun County. In 2014, President Ditzler and a small planning committee created the Albion Scholars program, in which up to 10 students a year who are qualified for admission to Albion College, and who were educated for at least three years in the Albion school district, and graduated from Marshall High School would receive full four-year scholarships as well as room and board. The planning committee also decided to open the program to students of any ethnic group who were from low-income and uneducated families. In return, these students would spend summers doing volunteer work on projects to enhance the community's development. The memorial scholarship fund that my wife and I established is now designated to help fund this new initiative. Seven students were selected in its first year, one white and the others black, an extremely impressive start, and it seems so far that all but one of these will be able to meet the academic challenge of Albion College. Now called the "Build Albion Fellows Program" it is now in its third successful year of operation, and I have become a supporter.

My ties to the University of Michigan also grew stronger. In 1997, following several long estate planning sessions with the attorney helping us, we were advised that we should establish revocable trusts to protect our assets after our deaths. We had amassed a substantial collection of both African art and works by major American black artists. We also had one son who was mentally disabled and would require a lifetime of residential custodial care, and another son who had suffered several psychotic breakdowns and might also require our financial support indefinitely. We eventually decided that first we would donate our entire art collection to the University of Michigan Museum of Art. This greatly enhanced the museum's collection, and the Curtis Gallery of African Art was named in recognition of our gift. The prominent black American artists represented in our collection included principally Jacob Lawrence, with whom we had become friends shortly after our move to New York, as well as Charles Alston, who had been one of Lawrence's early mentors at the WPA's Harlem Community Art Center, and Beauford Delaney, also of that era. Our collection at that time was appraised at approximately $1.6 million and was our first major gift to the university. We also donated $250,000 to curate the collection, and gave art objects to U-M's Center for Afroamerican and African Studies (now the Department of Afroamerican and African Studies), along with a collection of U.S. stamps and commemorative coins and medals identified with black Americans. We gave a $1 million trust award to the School of Music, Theater, and Dance because black artists had always been substantially represented on its faculty, several of whose members were scholars in various areas of black music. These funds provide scholarships for students doing graduate work in black music.

But it is the University of Michigan School of Social Work that has been the principal recipient of our gifts. As of 2015, the school had been ranked either number one or two in its discipline by *U.S. News & World Report* for the past 15 years and in the top three for the past 30. Paula Allen-Meares, a black woman, was its dean from 1993 to 2008. She and my wife were friends and she visited us often on her trips to New York. Vivian was not only a proud graduate of the school, but also one of the New York metropolitan area's leaders in social work and a faculty member of almost all of its social work schools because their students were sent to the Kings County Hospital for their field placement year. On one of Dean Allen-Meares's visits, she mentioned that the school had lost a significant portion of its federal grant funding for a year and asked for our support. We agreed and made our first donation, for $1 million. Dean Allen-Meares added more than another million from department funds in 2007 to remodel a major portion of the school's basement floor for the home of the Vivian A. and James L. Curtis School of Social Work Research and Training Center, named in recognition of our gift. I added another $1 million a few years later, after Laura Lein succeeded Allen-Meares as dean, for improvements at the center and for endowed scholarships.

A renovation of the Curtis Center was completed in 2015, making it still more attractive. Its research support and program evaluation activities are united by a common mission: to eliminate mental health and health care access disparities so that underserved populations can live longer, healthier, and more productive lives. The center is supported financially by a mix of private philanthropy, School of Social Work funds, and income generated by the evaluation of sponsored projects. Undergraduate students, doctoral and postdoctoral candidates, and faculty members all use the center's facilities to pursue their work. Research support services include consultation on research design and statistical methods, pilot project funding, and awarding postdoctoral fellowships and doctoral travel grants. The Curtis Center Program Evaluation Group, the largest unit of its kind in the country, is directed by Sue Ann Savas and offers services such as course work, field placement, paid work, training and education series events, and program evaluation services to local, state and national entities.

Altogether, we have donated more than four and a half million dollars to the University of Michigan. This is because the university played such a major role not only in our own professional development, but also in the professional development of minority, women, and low-income students throughout its long history. On May 3, 2014, I had the honor of being awarded the degree of honorary doctor of science by the University of Michigan for my contributions to the field of medicine and the advancement of affirmative action within it. Albion College had awarded me the honorary degree of doctor of science in 1992.

THE YEARS SINCE I retired from Harlem Hospital and the Columbia University faculty have been among the busiest and most productive of my life. They have given me time not only to reflect on the course and meaning of my own life, but to come to a new realization of what the future holds for African-Americans in our nation. The deaths of Vivian in August 2007 and our son, Paul, four months later, cast a huge shadow over all of these years, but I gained a deeper desire for compassionate involvement in our suffering world, which spurred a burst of charitable donations of both money and my professional skills—for example my involvement with Alma's Home for Girls I and II, an experience that has deepened my understanding of how difficult it is to develop a nonprofit corporation. We do not live in a nonprofit world, and there is too little support for nonprofit ventures. I do not believe it is possible to "do good" unless one becomes a partner with existing social institutions, with their greater resources, that support a mission similar to your own, and who will have a longer life than your own.

In retrospect, I could not have lived my life as I did were it not for the good fortune of my growing up in Albion, home of one of the nation's strongest small private colleges and a town which was extremely prosperous thanks to the then-growing automobile industry. Then I went to the University of Michigan, a world-class research university which benefited greatly from the prosperity of the automobile industry, and was one of the universities leading the way toward greater inclusion of women, blacks, and other minorities, a position which it still battles to maintain. My career in academic medicine would have been impossible without faculty members at the University of Chicago who gathered major philanthropic support for the desegregation of the nation's medical schools, which came to fruition in my own work at Cornell and Columbia.

Scientific leadership from our higher education system is essential in helping us face the global challenges which threaten our very survival, but governance structures in both our own nation and the world are still dominated by doctrines of violence and monopoly control by elites who rarely operate in the public interest.

I spent each of the first five summers after I returned to Michigan as a *locum tenens* professional. I worked temporarily with inmates needing mental health care in the state prison system, where it was hard to recruit psychiatrists as full time staff members. That experience totally immersed me in the reality that the mass incarceration of black men has destroyed many lives; it's alarming and disgraceful that a third of U.S. black men have a prison record by the time they're in their 30s, as do two-thirds of U.S. high school dropouts, which affects whole families, not just those incarcerated. Social class differences and income and wealth disparities were more pronounced among black men in prison than between blacks and whites.

For example, the rate of imprisonment for black men who had not gone to college increased two and a half times between 1979 and 1999, while for black college men it actually decreased. The Pew Foundation reported in 2007 that the black middle class was not reproducing itself but was instead suffering rampant downward mobility, with more than half its children failing to earn as much as their parents and more than a quarter falling to the bottom of the income ladder, a magnification of the trend among American families in general. This was the state of affairs stoking the liberal populist uprising that led to President Barack Obama's election in 2008 and his still more amazing reelection in 2012, despite a rising tide of right-wing populism and the cries of racists who resented the rise of a black middle class and policies like affirmative action. Hard economic times historically inflame racial and social class tensions, leading to political polarization and a paralyzed Congress, such as we have experienced in the Obama years.

This can make it appear as if we are going backward instead of forward, but matters are more complex than they seem. We have been in a state of crisis for the past four or five decades, with rapid and sudden changes in the social roles of men and women, blacks and whites, and rich and poor. Everything is in a state of flux, with young adults increasingly free of prejudice against gays, bisexual, lesbians, and transgendered people; same-sex marriage now the law of the land; women in the military seeing combat duty; interracial marriage rates on the rise, and biracial heterosexual and homosexual couples no longer embarrassed in public. A global economy has taken jobs away from working-class Americans, and advanced medical and dental procedures as well as professional technical jobs are performed more cheaply abroad than here. The time for change is approaching now that our nation has received the startling news that the suicide rate for middle-class whites now exceeds that of all other ethnic groups, including blacks and Hispanics.

The shrinkage of the Albion public school system since the year 2000 is an example close to my home of just how much the world has changed. The Bush administration's No Child Left Behind legislation forced public schools to repeatedly test all students and to hold teachers responsible if children failed to show improvement from year to year. It made no difference if their unemployed parents were demoralized and prone to self-defeating and often abusive behavior, hopelessly unable to provide a home life that was inspiring. Schools failing to show improvement were abandoned by students, who were free to transfer to better-performing schools, taking their state per-pupil allowance—a little over $7,000 in 2014 here in Michigan—with them. Unsupported claims were being heard that privatizing public education was the solution. It's the same old refrain: let the rich get richer and the poor will not get poorer. Albion's middle school children began going to Marshall in January 2016, leaving the town with only a K-5 school. The population of all the districts surrounding Albion is almost entirely white, but the more achievement-oriented black and white parents have been transferring their students to these nearby schools since the year 2000. Even citizens in those more prosperous districts were disgruntled about their school tax bill, so these districts have been sending their school buses to Albion to transport any children whose parents chose to transfer them to that district. In 2016, Michigan Department of Education statistics showed that more than 1,000 of Albion's school-age children were enrolled in nearby school districts, while fewer than 1,000 were attending school in Albion. I wish to point out that the students remaining in school in Albion, both black and white, are predominantly from low-income families and increasingly difficult to teach because of their emotionally and financially impoverished backgrounds.

Well, well, what do we have here? We have a nice case of increased racial and economic school integration, the likes of which had never been seen in those surrounding school districts. Black youngsters from Albion are generally more impoverished now than they were before the manufacturing companies that provided high employment and good wages left town. These youngsters now are welcomed in school districts near Albion which never had more than a few black residents, if any, and were absolutely known to be unfriendly to blacks, even when they were only driving through. Now these relatively poorer black children, and their state subsidies, are being welcomed with open arms. The black children attending those schools also behave better and learn better than they did in Albion, where the school-age population is increasingly dominated by low-income blacks and whites who share non-achieving behavior. Who said white people would never accept busing? This is a dramatic example of unintended consequences, and shows that we truly are living in a topsy-turvy period of American history. Sometimes success is hard to see even if you're looking at it.

I am reminded of when I used to take the Long Island Rail Road from my home in St. Albans, Queens, to my office near downtown Brooklyn. The train was often only half full when I got on at the St. Albans stop; at that point, almost all the passengers were white, and whites and blacks sat as far apart from each other as possible, as if their behavior were being controlled by a racially stereotyped scenario. The train suddenly filled up at the next stop, Jamaica Terminal. When the doors opened there, the mostly white commuters scrambled onto the train as fast as they could and quickly sat next to anyone, regardless of whether their neighbor was white or black or Asian or whatever.

The same scenario played in reverse on the return trip, since the train filled up fast at Atlantic Avenue where the commute began. What I learned from this was that race prejudice is a luxury which can be dropped quickly when it's no longer the best option: skin color means less when a train is crowded.

I often observe the same phenomenon while riding on the subway, or a bus, train, or plane. The person sitting next to me, white or Asian or Hispanic, will say nothing until some incident occurs to break the ice and we begin a conversation, which will go on for a while if we find some common interest. By the end of the trip, we will usually be relating to each other as persons rather than as stereotypes. On one plane ride, I sat next to a Japanese businessman and his daughter, and at the end of our trip I was invited to visit them as a guest in their Tokyo home. On other occasions, whites have invited me to their homes here in America, and my wife and I exchanged visits several times with a German couple we met years ago.

Ever since increasing numbers of black people began moving to other parts of the country from the rural South, the real estate industry has made a nice profit by encouraging whites to leave their neighborhoods as soon as blacks moved in. Federal, state and city governments worked along with the banking and insurance industries to red-line neighborhoods, leading to neighborhood segregation and the whole retinue of ills that follows it. They knew that whites would be willing to pay a premium to live in a safe neighborhood with good schools and businesses that catered to their needs, and they steered blacks into already black neighborhoods where the quality of goods and services was a different story. Since home ownership is usually the single greatest source of family wealth, perpetuating this arrangement meant that the wealth and income differentials would continue indefinitely. The flight to the suburbs led to the death or decline of most of our great cities, and urban renewal plans have never gained much political traction due to the dominant group's incentives to maintain the status quo. President Nixon appointed former Michigan Governor George Romney as Secretary of Housing and Urban Development in 1969, and he was sincerely dedicated to the desegregation of American suburban life. However, this was not one of the President's priorities. Often thwarted by Nixon, Romney resigned after Nixon's reelection. When President Obama announced an initiative that revived the idea of desegregating the country's suburbs, he was immediately denounced and vilified.

Here again, the situation may be better than it first appears. As income and wage growth stagnates, younger Americans began to find the underpriced real estate in ghetto neighborhoods attractive. In Washington, D.C., for example, property near Howard University, with an enrollment of 10,000 students and long the most powerful of black higher educational institutions, became increasingly interracial and expensive; when significant numbers of middle-class whites and blacks moved to the surrounding suburbs, they left behind real estate that young whites soon occupied. In New York City, real estate prices in formerly all-black neighborhoods have reached stunning heights.

All of this certainly stunned the extremely talented and renowned film director Spike Lee, whose seven-minute, foul-mouthed tirade against white gentrification became famous. Here is the angry message he unleashed in an address to an interracial audience during African American History month in 2014: why is it that it isn't until a lot of young whites move into Harlem or Bedford-Stuyvesant or the South Bronx that you begin to get better police protection, that you get garbage picked up every day, that you get improved schools, that you begin to get fancy restaurants where you couldn't find one before, that there's a Starbucks on every corner, and upscale stores selling high-priced goods? It's true that some of those young whites are hippies or artists looking for empty spaces that are cheap. Black people living in those neighborhoods are expected to stop having parties and playing loud music because the police are called to quiet them down. At the time he said all this, a story in the *Wall Street Journal* pointed out that Spike Lee was disingenuous, that he himself had been guilty of a kind of gentrification of his own. After making millions with his hit films, he sold the Washington Park townhouse he had bought for $650,000 to a white couple for more than a million, and then moved to a 9,000-square-foot palace on Manhattan's Upper East Side, which he bought from Jasper Johns for $16 million and later put on the market for an asking price of $32 million. Others noted that New York City neighborhoods have always been changing, so it should not be surprising that Harlem is now in play, and Detroit has recently begun to gentrify and gain new life. In other words, we are experiencing urban renewal of a kind that politicians never would or could undertake, and it is fueled by demographic and intergenerational attitudinal changes that don't follow a timetable. This is but another example that politicians rarely succeed in bringing about favorable social change because it is usually seen as a threat to the status quo, but if money is to be made, the rules of the game change suddenly. Shouldn't Spike Lee be glad to see his old neighborhood improve, and does it really matter if it is for what might seem to be the wrong reasons?

Meanwhile, the mass migration of people around the world is a problem which defies easy solution, not only in the European Union but also in the United States, where an explosive growth in the Hispanic population has made them, rather than African-Americans, the largest group of minority Americans. The African-American population now includes not only the native-born and immigrants from the Caribbean, but also from West Africa. One of President Lyndon Johnson's lesser hailed achievements was the passage of the Immigration and Nationality Act of 1965. National policy since the 1920s had been to enforce immigration quotas based on country of origin, which favored northern and western Europeans over southern and eastern ones and effectively excluded Asians and Africans. Blacks admitted now include large numbers of Nigerians; many of whom are poor but many others are among the most highly educated of our country's new citizens. One of the first acts passed by the United States Congress after the ratification of the Constitution limited immigration to "free white persons," mostly because they feared the entry of Haitians, who had ousted the French from their island to become the first majority black republic in history. Our nation's long legacy of racism is still far from outgrown, and the vestiges of African-American slavery still leave all persons of color vulnerable to mistreatment as members of a semi-caste system, even one who rises to the office of President of the United States. We are, however, at the beginning of a promising conversation about changing race relations in this country. If only we were as far along in talking about the social class system that diminishes the future of many millions more of the world's financially disadvantaged citizens, or of the worldwide oppression of black people anywhere on earth, or of worldwide oppression of women, or of religious and ethnic fanaticism leading to genocidal threats and actions. Only responsible international governance can deal with these threats to world survival.

My optimistic frame of mind has been important throughout my life and I was born at just the right time of world history and the history of my country to a family of black sharecroppers in rural Georgia, who themselves had been born into a condition of "slavery by another name." I retired with the title of Clinical Professor of Psychiatry (Emeritus) of the Columbia University College of Physicians and Surgeons, having been Director of Psychiatry at Harlem Hospital Center in New York's Central Harlem for 18 years. This was one of the five medical schools which I served as a faculty member during my academic career. Perhaps the capstone of my career were my 12 years at Cornell Medical College as Associate Dean and Associate Professor of Psychiatry, during which time I led the affirmative action program which successfully desegregated that previously almost all-white school and helped it become what is now one of the most successfully racially integrated schools nationally, not only for students but also for faculty and administrators.

It was during those years that I published my first book, *Blacks, Medical Schools and Society* (1972), documenting the first wave of national affirmative action programs. In those years, I also served as a board member and later chairman of the board and president of National Medical Fellowships, a foundation which provided financial support with funds from major foundations and corporations to all medical schools in proportion to the effectiveness of their affirmative action programs. I spent the first few years after my retirement in 2000 completing a follow-up book, *Affirmative Action in Medicine: Improving Health Care for Everyone,* published in 2003 by the University of Michigan Press. In that book, I compared a random sample of 2,000 underrepresented minority medical school graduates with a similar sample of 2,000 nonminority medical school graduates for 25 years after they received their degrees in 1969 through 1973. It showed that, in the mid-1990s, the minority medical school graduates were primarily practicing in racially segregated neighborhoods like those from which they came and the nonminority medical school graduates were practicing primarily in middle-income neighborhoods like those from which they came.

This is a reflection of the continuing social segregation of the America in which we live and also shows the necessity for all social groups of our nation to enjoy equal protection of the law. It is a simple reflection of the sociological fact that graduates of medical schools, like graduates in many other professions, tend to retain the social support networks of their families of origin, and often will seek out those professionals even if their offices are located downtown and away from the original neighborhood. Blacks now constitute about 7 percent of medical school enrollment, a vast improvement over the 2 percent figure before affirmative action, but far from the 12 percent of blacks in our overall population. This simply documents the inferior public education blacks receive in their neighborhoods. Compare this with the representation of women in medical schools, which was only 8 percent before affirmative action but is now 50 percent. That's because women generally receive educations comparable to the men in their neighborhood. Moreover, women are beginning to outstrip men generally in higher education due to the adverse effects of the decline of manufacturing and other traditional male jobs in the United States. All areas of American professional life—law, engineering, business administration, and all fields of science and technology—are becoming more accessible to both sexes. Separate higher education systems for men and women, blacks and whites, and religious denominations are becoming things of our past. I never dreamed that in my lifetime I would see a black president, with his black first lady and two lovely daughters. It was a dream for me and a nightmare for a minority of others. Our nation is now in 2016 struggling with increasing mortality rates and an epidemic of alcohol and drug abuse among young and middle-aged white American men, in rage and despair over the loss of their previously superior social status. Their rates of depression, substance abuse and premature mortality exceed the rates among black and also Hispanic men, who had had no ethnic advantage to lose.

But we have come to a point of crisis in world history, which only a massive change in human behavior can resolve, and students of human behavior have a crucial role to play in seeking ways to help us help rather destroy ourselves. Our global advances in science and technology and even representative government have greatly reduced the violent warfare and oppression of previous centuries, as students of human behavior, history and economics like Stephen

Pinker, Robert Fogel, and others have shown, but our global problems now far exceed our existing national governments' ability to solve them. One such problem is uncontrolled population growth. There were fewer than a billion of us in 1800, and now there are more than 7 billion, the total having tripled in the past 60 years. While capitalism, especially in a controlled form as in China, has lifted more people out of poverty in five decades than anyone could ever have believed, we are still far from having an international governing body with the authority to plan, monitor and control the equitable distribution of resources for all the people of the world. While there is enough human intelligence in the world to solve this problem with existing resources of land, sea, water, and breathable air, we are close to destroying the delicate ecological balance of our planet, which provides a viable environment for all life forms. The United States insists on having veto power over all other nations, and our self-centered delusion is matched by approximately another 20 nations, all of whom have nuclear arsenals, chemical and biological weapons of war, and computer technology which can cripple other nations at will. We now have 20 (some estimate it may be as many as 30) other nations who are vying with us to be considered exceptional, and to bring about total destruction of the planet and its delicate ecosystem.

Although we have the intellectual power to prevent our destruction, we have so far shown a lack of worldwide moral power to conquer our primitive addiction to brute force to solve inevitable human conflict. It is my optimistic hope that effective international, national, and regional governmental authorities, utilizing scientific method rather than brute force and withholding knowledge and power from others, will prevail in the short term. My optimism is mixed with a realistic awareness that there are obvious limitations on the ability of human intelligence to solve all of our problems. For example, we know that we live in a visible and predictable world which can be understood by Newtonian physics, but the subatomic world of quantum physics is totally beyond human understanding; in that world, a thing can be in two places, or even everywhere, at once, and we cannot understand the nature of time and space and energy in the vast reaches of interstellar space. It is enough to keep us humble and make us understand how much we need each other. It is a good feeling to read journals like *Science* and *Scientific American* and see that nowadays articles rarely carry the name of only one author; there may be more than 20, and they come from research centers in many nations as well as both great universities and small colleges, because scientists speak a common language to solve common problems. It is not only a challenge but also a great time to be alive: there could be no better time to devote one's life to the study of human behavior. From the beginning of my career through the series of crossroads and roadblocks encountered, I have repeatedly met and been enabled by persons coming not only from my own group but other groups as well who were willing to form relationships with me on the basis of our common humanity despite our differing groups of origin. Ralph Waldo Emerson's philosophy was influenced in many ways by the Hindu and Buddhist beliefs that we are not separate from but a part of all life forms as part of a delicate planetary ecosystem, and that "the heart and soul of all men being one, this bitterness of his and mine ceases, his is mine, I am my brother, and my brother is me."

FIGURE 6-1. In 1992 I was awarded an honorary Doctor of Science Degree by Albion College for my work in the field of medicine.

FIGURE 6-2. Vivian and me with Albion College President Mel Vulgamore.

PROGRAM

~

WELCOME AND INTRODUCTIONS
Paula Allen-Meares
Dean and Professor, School of Social Work

REMARKS
Jorge Delva, PhD
Associate Professor of Social Work
and
Matthew O. Howard, PhD
Professor of Social Work and Psychiatry

PROVOST'S ACKNOWLEDGMENT
Lindsey Rossow-Rood
Director of Development

PRESENTATION OF PINS
and
CLOSING REMARKS
Paula Allen-Meares

RESEARCH CENTER TOUR
Kristine Siefert, PhD
Professor of Social Work

VIVIAN A. and JAMES L. CURTIS

Vivian A. (MSW '48) and James L. Curtis (MD '46) have been involved in a number of activities across U-M's campus in the years after they graduated. Contributors to LSA, the School of Music, and the U-M Museum of Art, their most recent donation to the School of Social Work to endow a scholarship fund for MSW and PhD students, recognizes and honors Vivian's career and affection for the school. To acknowledge the Curtises' generous gift, the School's research center has been renamed the Vivian A. and James L. Curtis School of Social Work Research and Training Center.

The Curtises met in 1948 at Wayne County General Hospital, where Vivian conducted her field placement in psychiatric social work and James was in the first year of his psychiatric residency training. They married the following year and moved to New York City, where he pursued his career in academic psychiatry and she began her social work career.

Vivian held faculty appointments at many of New York's major universities. For 46 years she was on the social work staff of Kings County Hospital, the largest unit of the New York City hospital system, and the teaching hospital of the State University of New York Downstate Medical Center in Brooklyn. As director of the department of social work for 25 years, she and her staff supervised social work students from all of the New York schools of social work doing their field work placements in the medical, surgical, or psychiatric services. Vivian retired in 1995.

James Curtis retired in 2000 after nearly 20 years as director of psychiatry at Harlem Hospital. An emeritus clinical professor of psychiatry at Columbia University's College of Physicians and Surgeons, he has written two books printed by the U-M Press: *Blacks, Medical Schools, and Society* (1971) and *Affirmative Action in Medicine: Improving Health Care for Everyone* (2003).

ABOUT THE CURTIS RESEARCH
AND TRAINING CENTER

The goal of the Curtis School of Social Work Research and Training Center is to foster interdisciplinary externally funded research to advance knowledge in the areas of mental health, substance abuse, and health. Research on the comorbidity of these problems will be a priority since the service needs of people affected by multiple problems are complex and challenging. Research on comorbidity has been relatively neglected until recently and has important implications for social work. The focus is on exciting, emerging areas of research in which the U-M SSW should be positioning itself. The Curtis Center will be co-directed by Professors Matthew Howard and Jorge Delva.

 Matthew Howard earned a BA and an MS in psychology from Western Washington University, and his MSW and PhD from the University of Washington. His research focuses primarily on substance use, abuse, and dependence, particularly in adolescents. He is conducting two NIDA-funded studies of cognitive and psychiatric problems in incarcerated adolescent ecstasy and inhalant users. He is also interested in juvenile delinquency and youth violence.

 Jorge Delva, a native of Chile, is a graduate of the University of Hawaii and a fellow of The Johns Hopkins University. He is a faculty associate with the Center for Social Epidemiology and Population Health in the School of Public Health, the National Institute of Mental Health Research Center on Poverty, Risk, and Mental Health in the School of Social Work, and the Survey Research Center at the Institute for Social Research (ISR), University of Michigan. His work involves using multi-level statistical techniques to study the effect and trends of individual risk and protective factors on substance use and childhood obesity while taking into account neighborhood and other contextual-level factors with a particular focus on racial and ethnic differences. Dr. Delva is the editor-in-chief of the journal *Social Work,* the flagship journal of the profession.

DEDICATION
OF THE

VIVIAN A. AND JAMES L. CURTIS
SCHOOL OF SOCIAL WORK
RESEARCH AND TRAINING CENTER

~

SATURDAY, May 5, 2007
1:00 P.M.

MCGREGOR COMMONS
SCHOOL OF SOCIAL WORK BUILDING

FIGURE 6-3. Vivian passed away in 2007. Earlier that year, in appreciation of a large financial donation to the University of Michigan School of Social Work, The Curtis Center for Research and Training was established.

FIGURE 6-4. My son Paul and me with School of Social Work Dean Paula Meares.

FIGURE 6-5. Receiving an Honorary Doctor of Science Degree from President Mary Sue Coleman of the University of Michigan in May 2014.

FIGURE 6-6. Attending the reception given at the School of Social Work with President Coleman (second to left), Dean Laura Lein (right), and Marian Swan Harper (left), who graduated from the University of Michigan Law School in 1950 and who was my girlfriend before I met my wife.

"Even As We Fight and Die"

James L. Curtis
Albion College 1942

I begin with the stories of two men.

Imagine that I am Edmond Van Osten, 31, of Brooklyn, N.Y. For nine years, I have been a sheet metal worker. The other day, I applied for work at the Brewster Plant, in Long Island City, which is handling a big defense contract. The personnel manager told me that there were no openings. A little surprised, I waited around and saw 35 or 40 other sheet metal workers hired. The next day, I went again to the Brewster Plant, this time asking for a job as sheet metal helper. I was informed curtly that there were no openings for sheet metal helpers. Don't you think I'm qualified? No, they can't think that, for my references are good. Do I have a prison record? No, they can hardly suspect me of Fifth Column intentions.

The other story begs to be told. My name is Charles Ashe and I live in Washington, D.C. The newspapers announced some time ago that pilots were wanted to fly the U.S.-made bombers to Britain. There were the usual qualifications, such as having 400 hours in the air. As a fully qualified commercial pilot and a licensed air instructor with several thousand hours in the air, I applied to the Ferry Command. But something strange happened to me. Before I stated my qualifications, I was told that I could not serve. The next week, I received a letter from a Captain Mugford stating an additional requirement for the service. In simple finality, the requirement informed me that all applicants must be of the white race. Edmond Van Osten is also a Negro. A saboteur would have greater chance of being hired by the Brewster Plant than he.

How I wish it were not true of America—this report I am about to give. But does the truth ever hurt us really? And even now, actually in the war, must we be silent about the "breaches of democracy in our own land?" Not in disloyalty but rather truest patriotism, my answer is, "Now is not the time to be silent." It is patriotism with an eye that looks beyond the crisis—a patriotism which could, in the peace to come, protect this land of ours from a recurrence of the Hitlerism it is pledged to destroy.

American wartime industry will set the stage for the first act in our drama. It is an industry which calls to workers in the trades and skills. There is a call, too, for thousands of workers to do a common labor. The Anaconda Wire and Steel Company of Hastings, New York, ends its call for labor with this warning: "No Italians, Germans, *or Negroes.*" But no, I say to myself, they don't mention Negroes in the same breath as Italians and Germans. We're at war with Italy and Germany. Negroes are completely, absolutely American. Did not a Negro poet cry out:

"And never yet, oh haughty land,
When that fair flag has been assailed,
For men to do, and men to die
Have we faltered or have failed . . ."

Do you think I have cited an exceptional instance? I wish it were, but from the recent report of the American Youth Commission, we learn that many employers with substantial armament contracts have been "blatant and unashamed" in refusing to hire Negroes, no matter how competent or well trained.

Last summer, Negroes planned to march on Washington 50,000 strong in a gigantic protest to this nation's blind suicide. They planned on until the president issued executive order No. 8823 setting up a Fair Employment Practices Committee. This committee was to put an end to racial discrimination on the part of companies holding defense contracts. But who can rebuild a temple in three days? Referring to New York City, *Time* magazine reports that of 1,400 Negroes recently trained for defense work, only 70 got jobs.

Nothing short of a miracle could have saved America this embarrassment. Since 1865, there has been time for executive orders against discrimination; there has been need of fair employment practices. It takes a war—and then it is too late.

The next act of our drama takes us into the armed forces of this country.

One of every ten of the draftees will be, by accident of birth, a Negro. These men are asked to fight, these men *will* fight, to save a democracy they have never had. "Fight," their own leaders tell them, "for a chance to build a democracy." Those leaders were black doughboys in 1917. They had gone to France "to do the chambermaid work of the American Expeditionary Force," as a writer in *Scribner's Commentator* characterizes it, and to build bridges and dig trenches for white soldiers. But with the coming of the poison gas and the shrapnel of the Meuse Argonne, there came also a most impressive, democratic equality. It died with the armistice.

In this war, we got off to a flying start by sending Negro draftees to train in the South. And so far as those draftees were concerned, the day they crossed the Mason and Dixon line their war was declared. Disgraceful evidence of this fact was found one April morning at Fort Benning, Georgia. Clad in the uniform of the United States Army, Private Felix Hall was found hanged to death from a tree. As of this morning, the War Department has not found a clue to the murderers.

At Camp Robinson, Arkansas, Donald Curry, a white lieutenant, was drilling a squad of Negro soldiers down the state highway. Suddenly, a band of state troopers and armed civilians appeared and told Curry to get his niggers off the road and into the ditch. Curry was too slow about it and was slapped and cursed as a "nigger-lover" and a "damn Yankee." That evening, the camp was invaded by an armed band. Through all of this, the Negro soldiers were defenseless; no guns had been issued to them. After these incidents, almost half of them went AWOL. I would not be one to say that there was less soldierly spirit in those who deserted.

The Catholic magazine *Commonweal* spoke out in a brave, clear note. "Segregation of Negro troops from white troops produces a host of evils. It makes impossible that three-musketeer sort of solidarity. It encourages the giving of better quarters and facilities to white outfits. It encourages the fear of arming the Negroes, making them helpless to protect themselves short of insurrection or desertion." Of course, the Army cries out that is impracticable, even when a volunteer interracial division is suggested by both blacks and whites, including a fraternity of young white college men at the University of North Carolina.

The scene shifts. We are at Pearl Harbor, December 7, 1941. The battleship Arizona is attacked. Its crew resists valiantly. "A Negro mess-attendant who never before has fired a gun on the ship mans a machine gun on the bridge

until his ammunition is exhausted. He is one of the last men to leave the ship."
That story, reported *verbatim* from a naval officer, means a great deal more
than it seems.

The United States Navy refuses to advance any Negro beyond the rank of
messman. Therefore, most intelligent and proud young Negroes are system-
atically excluded from their country's navy. Even now, with urgent pleas for
young men to enter the marines, the navy, or the naval reserve, the navy has
announced officially, to the Negro press, that it has not changed its policy in
regard to Negro enlistees.

It is a month later, January 3, in Madison Square Garden. Joe Louis comes
into the ring to risk the heavyweight championship of the world in a fight
for naval charity. This man's navy would accept Louis's purse of $60,000, but
would not accept Louis himself as anything but a dishwasher.

And the Air Corps, the newest of our military branches—what of it? Only
after the hardest fight was concession grudgingly made as a pre-election move.
At first, the Negro squadron-to-be was at Chicago and was a joke for its lack
of equipment. Later, a Jim Crow squadron was placed at Tuskegee Institute.
According to latest reports, there is provision to train just sixty Negro cadets.

And with an ingenuity which might better be put to use against our country's foes, Negroes are excluded from every other air base for training. Secretary of War Stimson has dreams of a 2,000,000-man air force, but his sleep is
not disturbed by the fact that only 10 to 12 young Negroes are inducted into
the air training course every five weeks. There is *no room* for more.

You have seen some of the thousands of posters all over the land on which
Uncle Sam, with compelling eyes, calls on every red-blooded American to
fight in his army, navy, or air corps. I have stood before such a poster as one of
Uncle Sam's darker nephews, as have thousands of my fellows. How can Uncle
Sam look at us without lowering his eyes in shame? And is it any wonder that
a recent national conference of Negro leaders were regretfully forced to vote
overwhelmingly that Negroes are not unreservedly behind the war effort?

It is not my desire to make a stock indictment of the American social order. It is mine only to show to you the blighting inconsistency and hypocrisy
which is hindering our war effort for no good cause. And to say that there
was never a better time for my America to give the lie to the enslavement
of the bodies and spirits of men wherever it is found. Enlightened people
everywhere must listen to the reasonable demand of intelligent Negro opinion for the right to live as we are asked to fight and die. Beside the V sign of

victory abroad, we must hoist another V for victory at home. No more Negro technicians in industry shall be insulted by being forced to use their calculus to empty waste baskets. Our lily-white Navy shall match the Americanism of a Joe Louis. Our Army and Air Corps shall realize that Jim Crow strategy cannot win true freedom for the world. We must say "all these things that cry aloud to be said, even as we fight and die."

INDEX

Note: Page numbers in italics refer to figures.

Pakistan, 140

patriotism, 168

Pearl Harbor, 32, 169–70

Pensacola, Fla., 2, 11

Perkins, Dr. Marvin, 81–83, *91*

Petoskey, Mich., 36

Pew Foundation, 153

pharmaceutical industry, 126

Philadelphia, ix, 95

Philippines, 140

philosophy, JLC's guiding, 71

Phipps, Miss Nema, 31

Phoenix House, 138

Pinker, Stephen, 160–61

Pitts, Dr. Robert, 93

Pittsburgh Courier, 4

Plato, 62

Plessy v. Ferguson (1897), x, 108

police, 3, 127

polio, 51

Pontiac, Mich., 49, 51

Potter, Dr. Howard, 50, 63, 72

Poussaint, Dr. Alvin, 99

Powell, Lewis, 96

pragmatism, xii

pregnancy, 18; expectant fathers and, 68–69; out-of-wedlock, 16, 17, 147

Presbyterian Church, 77–78

pride, instilled by completing chores, 11–12

Princeton Theological Seminary, 77

private practice, JLC's, 72, 73, 82

Protestants, 74, 82, 84, 143. *See also names of Protestant denominations*

Provident Clinical Society (Bedford-Stuyvesant), 78, 79

Provident Hospital (Chicago), 40

psychiatric treatments, 52–53

psychiatry, 57, 65: as JLC's career choice, 42, 50; JLC's Wayne County General Hospital residency in, 51–59; desegregation of, 50, 60

psychoanalysis, 52, 63, 73; of JLC by Dr. Bernard, 60, 61, 63

psychotherapy, 50–51, 126

psychotropic drugs, overuse of, 126

publications and speeches of JLC: *Affirmative Action in Medicine* (2003), 99, 103, 105, 109, 110, 111, 159; *Blacks, Medical Schools and Society* (1972), 105, 159; "Even As We Fight and Die" (1942), 33, 167–71; "Intravenous Drug Users and Human Immunodeficiency Virus Testing and Counseling—Reply" (1989), 132–33; "A Plan to Promote Professional Careers for Negroes" (1965), 80; "A Psychiatric Study of 55 Expectant Fathers" (1955), 68–69

public transportation, integration of, 154–55

Puerto Rico, Puerto Ricans, 78, 105, 118, 119

quantum physics, 161

Queens, 122, 138; JLC's home in St. Albans area of, *87*, 145, 154

race, racism, 16, 35, 59, 155, 157; biology and, 37; blood drives and, 40–41; in Brooklyn, 72–73; Du Bois and, ix, xi, xii; equality and, 78; integration and, 100; riots and, ix, 95; slurs and stereotypes of, 65, 101, 155; in World War II, 167–71

radicals, 76, 93, 102, 103

Rado, Dr. Sandor, 61–62

Randolph, A. Philip, 32

CPSIA information can be obtained
at www.ICGtesting.com
Printed in the USA
FSOW04n0726041217
41819FS